NIGHTLANDS

NIGHTLANDS

NIGHTLANDS

Nordic Building

Christian Norberg-Schulz

The MIT Press
Cambridge, Massachusetts
London, England

© 1996 Massachusetts Institute of Technology
This work originally appeared in Norwegian under the title
Nattlandene: Om byggekunst i Norden
©1993 by Gyldendal Norsk Forlag A/S
Photographs ©1993 by Christian Norberg-Schulz
Translation by Thomas McQuillan

This book was set in Garamond 3 and Mona Lisa Solid by Graphic Composition, Inc., and
was printed and bound in the United States of America.

Library of Congress Cataloging-in-Publication Data

Norberg-Schulz, Christian.
      [Nattlandene. English]
      Nightlands : Nordic building / Christian Norberg-Schulz ; translated by Thomas
McQuillan.
          p.   cm.
      Includes bibliographical references and index.
      ISBN 0-262-14057-8 (hc : alk. paper)
      1. Vernacular architecture—Scandinavia.   2. Architecture—Psychological
aspects—Scandinavia.   3. Vernacular architecture—Baltic Sea Region.   4. Architecture—Psychological aspects—Baltic Sea Region.   I. Title.
NA1201.N6713   1996
720′.948—dc20   95-38801
                                                                                  CIP

Contents

><->-o-<-I-<

Urnes Stave Church, Norway

This book is not a history of architecture; its object is not to account for the development through time of Nordic building, nor to catalog its most important manifestations. Its aim, rather, is to examine what Nordic building truly is, and this is best achieved by contrasting it with its counterpart: the classical architecture of the South. Insofar as the North and the South have throughout centuries upheld a relationship of interaction called the "European," any examination must also address the manner in which the North has assimilated "foreign" influence.

The names *North* and *South* denote geographical identities, so that when we speak of Nordic building, we imply that place acts as a starting point for discussion. It has long been recognized that place is integral to man's sense of form; this theme was introduced in Heinrich Wölfflin's book *Italien und das deutsche Formgefühl* (1931), but sank subsequently into oblivion, perhaps as a result of the increasingly international character of architecture before and after World War II, perhaps because historians sought to account for the formal mainly as a result of social conditions. By 1954, however, Sigfried Giedion called for a "new regionalism," and in the last decades reaction against international architecture has grown markedly stronger.

Giedion found the origins of new regionalism in Finland, thus a book on Nordic building is especially relevant. As a student of Giedion, it is natural that I continue the examination I began in *Between Earth and Sky* (1978) and *Genius Loci* (1979), and developed further in *The Concept of Dwelling* (1985). That I now investigate the significance of place in a book on Nordic building is a result of both a love for the particular part of the world to which I belong and because I feel that this work can shed light on issues of a general interest.

The method employed is phenomenological; that is, I do not seek to explain buildings as a result of influences, nor do I arrange them within a chain of stylistic developments, though of course both influence and style are significant realities. Instead, I consider building as it occurs as part of a local context and attempt to see it as it indeed is. This approach is grounded in the belief that buildings necessarily represent the world to which they belong, at times through a simple "participation," at others as a kind of "explanation." In general, we can assert that all buildings and settlements gather a world, and that we can only understand them in these terms.

When the world of a work of architecture is designated as local, it may seem as though inhabitants have been excluded from consideration; but this is only ostensibly so. The expression "life takes place" corroborates that life and place form a unit, and that a satisfactory analysis of place necessarily embraces that life which place admits. The phenomenological method is thus anything but detached from life; indeed, it gives us insight into the unity of life and place that psychological and sociological methods cannot. And because it is based in what things themselves are, it releases us as well from the cul-de-sac of semiology.

The phenomenological method is based on seeing. *Seeing* means, above all, recognizing something *as* something. When we visit a new place, we spontaneously recognize differences without being able to pinpoint what they consist. Recognition is obviously not a product of experience, but rather of a "fore-conception" that forms our basic manner of being. Although I cannot delve any deeper into this issue here, I must emphasize that this fore-conception allows for recognition of place as place. The life of place has thus as a precondition an original identity to which the term *the Nordic* refers.

It follows, then, that architecture is primarily specific to place, or domestic, but insofar as all particular places are manifestations of place in general, the domestic must be seen in relation to the universal and classical southern typologies. When I use the term *domestication,* I refer precisely to this interaction between the special, local and the general, imported. This does not imply support for nationalistic ideology but merely recognizes that all works of architecture are necessarily both rooted and universal.

This book, therefore, emphasizes folk architecture as a response to living in a specific place. Folk architecture arises in diverse regions as a result of specific methods of building. These methods are not merely due to available building materials and technologies but also to the desire to accommodate building to a local context. As such, the building traditions of the four Nordic countries have their origins in characteristic methods of building that have determined a sense of form that remains despite changes in technology and despite the arrival of the imported.

It follows from the above that works of architecture cannot be explained as expressions of social relations or as links in a stylistic chain, but they can only achieve their true significance in interaction with a place whose identity remains despite change. It is precisely in this aspect that international modernism failed and that the new regionalism of the North gains its relevance. For although the Nordic lands are also victims of contemporary loss of place, there nonetheless exists an undercurrent of work that provides a valid synthesis of the domestic and the foreign.

The plan of this book follows the proposed approach. The introductory chapter, "The Nordic," provides a tentative picture of the North as a given environment. The second chapter, "The Natural," exposes the natural roots and suggests how architecture can provide a response to naturally given conditions; thereafter follows a chapter wherein "The Domestic" is presented as a method and a tradition of building. "The Universal," which is present in Europe primarily in church building, is covered in a separate chapter, as is "The Foreign," which comprises formal and typological influences from the South. The nineteenth-century search for identity is discussed in "The National," while its converse, the participation in the new open world, is treated in "The International." The latter contains a critique of functionalism and defends the need for rooted architecture; this need is discussed in the final chapter, "The Regional." Here, the identities of the four Nordic lands are summarily characterized as variations of the common Nordic environment.

The book's subtitle, Nordic Building, has been chosen to emphasize that architecture is primarily something built, and that built form becomes an art when it gathers and represents the world to which it belongs. The Nordic art of building thus manifests what it means to "live poetically" under Nordic conditions, whereby the word *poetic* acknowledges the qualitative identity of the environment. From rooted medieval houses and wooden churches through the domestic classicism of the Renaissance and baroque, and national romanticism's echoes of the past to new regionalism's interpretations of the Nordic, such an art of building has been realized. Examples are legion, but this book has necessarily concentrated on the most characteristic. That the selection nevertheless corresponds for the most part to that found in conventional histories of architecture simply confirms its validity.

When I say that this book attempts to explain what the Nordic is, this also includes a desire to indicate a way out of postmodernism's dead end. For so long as building is isolated from the place to which it belongs, the result will necessarily remain inessential, despite any functionality. The result is indeed today's fragmented and meaningless surroundings. May an understanding of the Nordic art of building aid us in recovering a sense for wholeness and meaning.

Finally, I would like to thank Thomas McQuillan for his perseverance in all phases of this translation.

H. Egedius, *Music and Dance*

The Nordic

North and South are familiar names. When we use these terms, we think not of cardinal directions but of domains with character and identity. We travel from the North to the South to experience warmth and sun and all that this entails; we travel from the South to the North to—well, this is precisely the question! What is it that we find there? What is it that distinguishes the Nordic world?

We experience the North spontaneously upon arrival. Another mood envelops us, but we are not immediately aware of what has happened: is it light, is it the land itself, is it the vegetation, or is it the built environment that is somehow different? It is indeed all of these. Here in the North, the sun does not rise to the zenith but grazes things obliquely and dissolves in an interplay of light and shadow. The land consists not of clear massings and distinct spaces; it disperses as fragment and repetition in the boundless. The vegetation is not characterized by particular species, such as stone pine and cypress, but is instead network and thicket. And the buildings lose much of their figural effect; houses lie scattered and hidden. Moreover, they consist for the most part of wood, a material that lacks the permanency of stone. As a result, visitors from the South exclaim: "Look: here the houses are wooden!"

In that the North is composed of several and differing countries, it may appear pointless to speak of a "Nordic world." But while it is true that the Nordic lands are distinct, we can nonetheless group them under the common heading "the North." That this term is something more than a collective noun is evident; we have already suggested that it encompasses a region of character and identity. Perhaps the name itself can direct us? Whereas the etymology of "south" is linked to "sun," the sources of "north" are more obscure. It is cognate with "below" and "under," but what can this tell us? The Italian word for south is *mezzogiorno,* "midday," and the lands there, *il meridione,* are accordingly "lands of the sun." North, conversely, is *mezzanotte,* "midnight," and the lands there, *il settentrione,* receive their name from the seven stars of Ursa Major. These terms reveal that the cardinal directions are qualitatively experienced, and that day and night, sun and star confer character upon an environment.[1] Thus the North differs from the South. In the North, we are "below," in that we distance ourselves from the light that emanates from above, and the sky is no longer "high." It is as participants in an environment that inhabitants and their works bear evidence thereof. And it is precisely our task to indicate in what manner architecture reflects the given identity of an environment.

But as yet, northern identity has scarcely been understood. Interest has been concentrated on the South, birthplace of the Idea, the Form, whereas the North has been but a white fleck on the map. Even after the northern regions became integrated with the European whole, they remained unknown territory. This is not to imply, however, that the North has, through the ages, been isolated from the European community. Southern influence has been significant and has in many ways provided a yardstick

Porvoo, Finland

for the Nordic domestic. That is to say that Northern forms of expression are not locally explicable but must instead be understood as the result of the encounter of the domestic and the imported. As such, comparison with the South is integral to an understanding of what lies concealed in the name North.

As a point of departure for this comparison, we can examine that which gives an environment its primary character: *light*. An exhibition of Nordic painting, shown in the United States in 1982–83, was called "Northern Light."[2] For it is precisely light that defines the Nordic world and infuses all things with mood. Light informs us instantly that we are no longer in the South. "Light gives all things their presence," said (the American architect) Louis Kahn, and he meant not that light creates things, but that it defines their manner of appearance.[3] It is exactly this determinative effect that distinguishes Nordic light. That is, light manifests that space which things and life inhabit, and Nordic light thus creates a space of moods. In the North we occupy a world of moods, of shifting nuances, of never-resting forces, even when the light is withdrawn and filtered through an overcast sky.

The South, too, has its mood. Unquestionably. But there, all is stable; indeed, the South is marked by the single mood that becomes manifest when sunlight permeates space and encompasses all things. It would thus be misleading to designate the South as a world of moods. Gabriele d'Annunzio expresses the moodless environment in the poem "Meriggio,"

(Midday).[4] In it, he relates how all appears to pause when the sun reaches its zenith, how the environment becomes unified, eternal, and how life itself becomes "divine." Hence the extensity of southern space: sun saturated and homogeneously whole, it is limited only by the horizon and the vaulted sky. The morning brings the emergence of space, the evening its withdrawal, but with the sun directly overhead, space reveals itself as it in reality is.

Let us examine more closely what southern space means for people and things, in order that we might better understand the Nordic. In "sun-space," each thing becomes discrete, with its own form and distinct character. Thus Plato recognized the essence of the thing in its appearance, or *eidos*. Greek mythology appears, as well, as a community of "characters," that is, distinct. Homogeneous space itself found its theoretical expression in Euclid's geometry, if only indirectly. The Greeks, in fact, had no word for space; for them, space was self-evident, and thus it was unnecessary to name it. Nonetheless, the southern sun-space has always acted as a determinant for Mediterranean architecture, from the Greek definition of corporal presence to the Roman representation of space as such.[5]

Light, Skorve i Flatdal, Norway

It is unnecessary in this context to conduct an exhaustive analysis of the southern environment, but it must be emphasized that spatial homogeneity entails that a thing's eidos resides not merely in its limiting contour but also in its plastic-tactile substance. In the South, things appear as bodies, and as a result, Italians designate the fine arts "figurative." This desire for the figural is clearly expressed in their painting; whether one considers Renaissance or contemporary work, discrete objects occupy a homogeneous space.[6] Analogous qualities are found in other art forms as well. The *bel canto,* thus, is based on conspicuous, figural melodies, and Italian opera is essentially an interplay of characters. Even one's daily conduct has as its object to *far figura,* that is, to "show oneself," and at the same time to accept the extant, without demand for explanation. In this way, the individual is liberated for extroversion, and society becomes a meeting.[7]

In summary, we may say that the southern world constitutes a lucid whole in which each thing "knows" what it is. When we designate the South as classic, it is because it is exemplary. This is not, however, to state that it is static and binding, but that the freedom to perform implies instead each thing's potential as a power center, in accordance with Aristotle's concept of *energeia.* This is perhaps what d'Annunzio had in mind when he described life as "divine." That is, the divine finds expression in a whole that operates as complete and self-explanatory. In the South, biblical creation therefore appears fully achieved, in that each thing has its place, according to its kind. Classical architecture presents and maintains the southern world as homogeneous space, as characteristic plasticity, as distinct gestalt; and it is stone that provides its implicit permanence.[8]

We must measure the reactions of southerners visiting the North against this background, for they encounter a world that is hardly complete but rather unfinished and fragmentary. This is not to suggest that the Nordic landscape lacks strength or form, but that it rarely combines these qualities as a rounded gestalt. In his remarks on Finland, the architecture historian Sigfried Giedion expresses it thus: "Finland, covered with its network of lakes and forests, suggests in its structure the day of Creation, when water and earth were first separated."[9]

We might, in principle, extend this statement to include all Nordic lands. For it is as if these landscapes were in the process of becoming. This impression, of course, has nothing to do with agriculture or geology but with an incompleteness that suffuses its landforms. Even "charming" Denmark "meanders in hill and dale" yet lacks the larger features that characterize the cultivated landscapes farther south.[10] But it is in Norway that the anticlassical environment becomes most strongly manifest. One need only mention the infinite mountain plateaus, and even the Norwegian valley is extension rather than enclosed space.

Let us now, after these introductory characterizations of the Nordic environment, turn to a more systematic examination of northern space, its

Finnish landscape

Danish landscape

Norwegian landscape, Flatdal, Telemark

qualities of form, of gestalt. If we maintain that light defines the Nordic character, it is to imply that we understand "climate" qualitatively. Light is conjunctive with weather, and in the North, weather plays a more important role than in the South's more stable world. Its significance is evidenced not only in everyday modes of converse but also in many forms of speech. Thus both Danish and Norwegian use *opp i været* (up in the weather) to denote "up," an expression that demonstrates how the southern sky is transformed in the North by everchanging weather. The Norwegian *vær* (weather) is furthermore related to *å være* (to be). In the North, then, "to be" signifies being thrown into a changing and unpredictable world, that is, a world that provides no fixed point of view, a world in which we are unable to accept the given and act freely. In the North we are bound to a world of forces, because we inhabit the realm of the night. As sunlight fades, things lose their eidos, their identity; the world transforms into what the German poet Eichendorff has called *Weltgewimmel* and *Weltgewühl* (the world's teeming and turmoil).[11] Thus we are trapped in the web, the thicket, to which the forest belongs. Our fundamental tenor is dread, but a dread that also conveys a kind of freedom different from the South's conditional acceptance.

In spatial terms, this means that the homogeneity of the southern environment is cleft into fragments of disparate character. In one direction, the sky is perhaps clear and blue, in another it is occluded by dark clouds, while the zenith agitates unceasingly. Our only measure against this changeability is the steady rhythm of the seasons. We can never be sure of what the day may bring, but we know that spring will come, and we greet it as an "explanation." Suddenly, the soil begins to glisten; light, which saturates southern space, here seems to emanate from things themselves. They radiate in the white summer night, all is bewitched, the palpable dissolves in enigmatic shimmer. The night thus assumes the day's role: it is the time of the revelation of the thing's essence. We celebrate Midsummer Eve with bonfire and dance, for it is then that we experience the forces of nature at their most benign. The dangerous dark is nearly gone; things become nearly comprehensible in the summer night's diffuse half-light. But something analogous occurs in winter, too. In the North, it is only on winter nights that the sky becomes large, whole. Over the snow-covered earth it vaults, saturated with a peculiar "dark light." Finally, it is cupola and firmament; a greater order emerges, and we see that the North is truly a midnight world.[12]

Such is northern space: an unsurveyable manifold of places without fixed boundary or clear geometric form. Is it only night that can cull this diversity to wholeness, or can we find another coherence? The words "web" and "thicket" imply as much. Where things cannot appear individually but are interwoven, we occupy a state that can truly be called anticlassic. In such a place, it is not a thing's eidos that matters but its veiled relation to all others. The forest is therefore the most fitting image of the northern world. Deep and inscrutable, it is without direction for movement. Its space is tight but nonetheless boundless, its mood the passage of dawn to dusk. The for-

Clouds

N. Astrup, *St. Hans's Day Bonfire*

Forest path

Forest

Clearing

est's freedom is the freedom to abandon the path and hide away, and the path itself is a fitting image of northern existence.[13] It passes through heather and moss and leads always onward; it allows us to forget our outset, our destination. But it discloses the terrain as it is and brings us near to things. It is thus a course of discovery; indeed, Nordic existence lies precisely in this unceasing search for discovery, rather than in the consenting acceptance of the given.

It might seem to follow that the Nordic world is incomprehensible and without perceptible form. But we know that this is not so, and linguistic names corroborate that here, too, are "valley" and "mountain," "declivity" and "plain" recognized, recalled identities. It is simply that they are rarely rounded out in themselves but are rather engaged in a continuum we have designated "the web." To gain a foothold in this web, however, it is first necessary to create an opening in the thicket; and in fact, the Norwegian term *rom* (space, room) derives from *rydning* (clearing). In the North, then, space is not continuous and comprehensive but is an aperture that humans have created in the unsurveyable. As such, this space becomes a home, in that home is precisely a known place of dwelling in an unknown world. Thus says Saint-Exupéry, "I have discovered a great truth: to know that man dwells."[14]

Pond

Here, admittedly, he speaks of the need for dwelling in the desert, but as regards the need for dwelling, the extremes converge: both forest and desert require that space be delimited. It is only in the European South that space is given; thus Italian has no word for "home."

When mood and web replace divine character and plastic corporeality, things dissolve. They become dematerialized and fluid, or emerge as *trolls,* indefinite creatures that belong to no particular species. In Greece, place was identified with a corresponding mythic god,[15] whereas northern *genius loci* is the *nisse* or *tomt,* as the Swedes say, a term that also means "site."[16] Troll and nisse personify natural forces—not those distinct characters that advance in sunlight but occult things that emerge in the darkness of the night. That is why trolls burst when the sun shines upon them.

Waterfall

In the Finnish national epic, *Kalevala,* the Nordic world receives its strongest expression. Here are interwoven natural forces, divine manifestation, and the role of humans in a total, functioning world-picture that gave, upon its publication in the nineteenth century, an entire people an understanding of their identity.[17] This comes to the fore in the trial of strength between the old sage Väinämöinen and the young rationalist Joukahainen. It would be misleading to say that Joukahainen represents a southern, logical understanding; rather, he exhibits what results from the South's concrete grasp of reality when applied to the Nordic: a flattened and facile categorization:

Said the youthful Joukahainen,
"Many things I know in fullness,
And I know with perfect clearness . . .
From the rock springs forth the water,
And the fire from heaven descendeth,
And from the ore we get the iron
And in the hills we find the copper
Marshy country is the oldest
And the first of trees the willow
Pine-roots were the oldest houses
And the earliest pots were stone ones."

But Väinämöinen answers:

"Tell me words of deepest wisdom
Tell me now of things eternal!"

Joukahainen cannot, and draws his sword. But then

. . . Sang the aged Väinämöinen;
Lakes swelled up, and earth was shaken,
and the coppery mountains trembled,
and the mighty rock resounded.
And the mountains clove asunder;
On the shore the stones were shivered.

And Joukahainen sinks into the mire, until he must beg for his life.[18] The story demonstrates the meaning of a searching, Nordic discovery: it does not produce the thing but engages directly in it, partakes in the web, and thereby renders it comprehensible. When Väinämöinen sang the world, it achieved immediate presence, and logical order ended up in the swamp. The Nordic world demands just such a precognitive understanding. The *Kalevala* ends with Väinämöinen's death:[19]

Left his charming harp in Suomi
For his people's lasting pleasure,
Mighty songs for Finnish children.

It comes as no surprise that the *Kalevala* had great significance for music. Nearly all of Jean Sibelius's major works, which define Nordic musical art, were inspired by this national epic above all others. Sibelius not only realizes life and natural forces in sound, but he creates a music form that corresponds to the spatial structures described above. In his works, figural themes are not employed as a point of departure, and thus he does not produce characters that are exposed and developed as in classical music. Sibelius's characters remain undisclosed, fragments emerge and withdraw, scraps of "something" come to light and dissolve again. What is primary is mood, as rhythm (Third Symphony), or as atmosphere (*Tapiola*).[20] And even though characters remain hidden, they are nonetheless expressed as beings, for it is only that which *is* that may hide itself.

Despite the capacity for music to express the Nordic world, it is painting that manifests it most directly. Here, national differences come to the fore. As a result of the natural presence, landscape painting has had its greatest significance in the Nordic countries. This applies not only to Norway's drama but also to Denmark's charm. (Nature has indeed, since earliest times, marked ornamentation and decoration.) And as we have said, mood has formed Nordic painting's primary content, in that it follows from Nordic light.

In exploring how the Nordic is manifest in painting, it is appropriate to begin with Norway, where nature appears strongest and most immediate. Norwegian landscape painting gives direct expression to the environment previously described, above all in the work of Harald Sohlberg. His *Winternight in Rondane* is an unrivaled expression of the Nordic winter's dark light, and he himself characterizes the world thus given presence as "genuine and inexplicable":

> The endless plain upon which I stood was bathed in half-light and mysterious shadow. I saw deformed, twisted and overturned trees, mute indications of nature's inconceivably powerful forces, for the storm's might and fury. Now all lay calm and still: the stillness of death. I could hear my own rapid breathing. Before me in the distance rose a range of mountains, beautiful and majestic in the moonlight, like petrified giants. The scene was the most magnificent and filled with fantastic stillness that I have ever experienced. Over the white contours of a Nordic winter stretched the sky's endless vault, filled with myriad glimmering stars. It was like a holy service in a great cathedral."[21]

But Sohlberg could render the summer night's mystery as well: in the painting *Flowering Meadow in the North* (1905), the light that seems to radiate from the objects themselves fashions the mood. It is an atmosphere that encompasses the entire picture and expresses a world more suggestion than presence, where we are bewitched and drawn into nature's unfathomable continuum.

Nature's significance for northern inhabitants is demonstrated with intense empathy by Halfdan Egedius, who in the course of a short life affected the Nordic perception of the unity of life and place. In both *Barn Dance* (1895) and *Play and Dance* (1896), the action transpires in the darkness. Here, it is not body language that is of import but fantastic glimpses of something that remains undefined. In both paintings, Egedius seems to

H. Sohlberg, *Flowering Meadow in the North*

H. Sohlberg, *Winternight in Rondane*

want to tell us that life has darkness at its center, exposed with frightening intensity in celebration. In the former picture, the scene is enacted against a distant ground of spring sun. Again, it is darkness that is really light.[22]

In Finnish painting from the turn of the century, the forces that conceal themselves within a mood find even more immediate expression. Albert Edelfeldt's *Kaukola Ridge at Sunset* (1889) renders water the dominant element, as one might expect in the "land of a thousand lakes." But rather than appearing deep, it reflects the sky and unites above and below in a whole replete with vibratory tension. Akseli Gallén-Kallela's forest pictures realize this tension in a web of trunk and branch, and his illustrations for the *Kalevala* personify inscrutable nature with anticlassic brutality. In his *Lemminkäinen's Mother* (1897), the contrast between the dark Tuonela River in the realm of death and the abstracted rays of the sun from above forms a counterpoint to the figures and deepens the picture's content: a Nordic conflict between darkness and light. As such, the picture's realism is only ostensible, and its true meaning remains undisclosed.[23]

On the other shore of the Baltic Sea in Svealand, Sweden's central region, all becomes milder. In the fertile oases around Lake Mälar, deep woods are distant, and the skies higher. In *The Clouds* by Prince Eugen, a cumulus cloud conveys the Nordic summer light. The painter's words inform us how weakened the divine sun seems here in the North: "I thought at first that the light effect which I needed to achieve in the middle could be attained with help from the sun, but this form turned out to be too small. It had to be a large circle, and it became a cloud."[24]

But in Prince Eugen's work, the darker tones of the Nordic world reverberate as well. *The Forest* (1892), thus, is a fascinating portrayal of the thicket's boundlessness and of the reality of dark light. Eugène Jansson transposes Prince Eugen's forest vision onto urban space in *Österlänggatan* (1904) and shows, in this painting and in others as well, the interplay of nature in the built environment in the North.

Above all, however, it is the Danish painter Vilhelm Hammershøi's work that best represents the unity of light, environment, and built form. Here, the introvert drama, found in Norwegian and Finnish painting, and still resonant in the Swedish, disappears. All is subdued, becomes still, intimate, and the world is clothed in nuanced grays. At the same time, things exist precisely and with clear identity, but they do not possess the character of *Gegenstand* with eidos-forming shadow, and thus they lack southern plastic presence. "Light graces things with ghostly levity," and the backturned figure, found in many of Hammershøi's pictures, gazes into a space dispersed in an emptiness where the simple seems concealed.[25]

It is interesting to note that German poet Rainer Maria Rilke was intrigued by Hammershøi and visited him in Copenhagen, with plans to write about his art. This interest was no doubt due to Rilke's untiring attempts to understand and interpret things, because "that which sleeps in

A. Edelfeldt, *Kaukola Ridge at Sunset*

Prince Eugen, *The Cloud*

V. Hammershøi, *Danish Village Street*

V. Hammershøi, interior

Norwegian tun, Mo i Rauland

us awakes in things.[26] This statement proposes a pantheistic attitude that corresponds to the Nordic unity of life and thing. When a Nordic person "says" or "sings" the world, like Väinämöinen, it means an understanding of its inner and outer relations, rather than the representation of things as individuals. Thus Rilke ends his *Ninth Elegy* with the query: "Earth, isn't this what you want: to resurrect in us invisibly?"[27] In the work of Hammershøi, "earth" rearises on the threshold between the seen and unseen. It is the Nordic earth that we meet here, in Danish guise, where all is intimate, still, and simple, yet nonetheless infinite: such are Hammershøi's pictures *Sun Rain* (1903) and *Landscape* (1905).

H. Egedius, *The Dreamer*

Painting brings us closer to the Nordic world and leads us toward Nordic architecture. It confirms that Nordic space is simultaneously closed and limitless, as we experience in forests and among skerries, and corroborates that Nordic form embodies tension rather than character. And finally, it shows how this unity is manifested always as mood. As a result, Nordic comprehension is based not on logical category but on the sense of dynamic interplay. In the North, we live among things instead of in confrontation with them. Our empathy, however, is not an immediate accepting identification but rather a searching ruminative absorption, such as seen in Egedius's *The Dreamer* (1895).

We have seen how literature, music, and painting maintain the Nordic world. The examples give us insight into what is implicit in the concept "the Nordic," as environment and life form. But this environment where "life takes place" needs to be clarified in more than word, tone, and color; it must also be built, in order that its inhabitants can truly know where their place is, and thereby achieve a durable sense of belonging. The word "durable" is significant because it intimates that all transformations, which are the signs of life, must be referred to something that remains, to be meaningful. And that which remains is, above all, *place.* Thus has *stabilitas loci* been acknowledged from the outset as a fundamental need. In order that place should remain selfsame throughout transformation, its *genius loci* must be conserved. Every place, every region, is significant, and it is our task to understand and respect this. It is only then that we may say that we *dwell,* in the deeper sense of the word. And respect and comprehension must be made visual; that is, to build and to dwell are inseparably conjunctive.

It is architecture's task to enable dwelling, and this task is satisfied by building in resonance with the given place. Understanding of place is consequently architecture's basis, though this does not involve nearsighted focusing upon the local. The imported can serve as a measure, or tool, for achieving a better understanding of the domestic. The following chapters examine the meeting of the domestic and the imported in Nordic architecture, but in order to give these propositions a fundament, it is necessary to say a few words about architecture in general.

P. V. J. Klint, Grundtvig Church, Denmark

A. Aalto, Säynätsalo City Hall, Finland

In his little book on the poet Hebel, Martin Heidegger explains architecture in these words: "The buildings bring the earth as inhabited landscape close to man, fixing the nearness of neighborly dwelling under the expanse of the sky."[28]

The word "buildings" here includes "house," "town," and "city," and Heidegger further clarifies that the "inhabited landscape" coincides with that manifold to which man belongs. "To bring the earth as [the] inhabited landscape close to man" means to visualize place as space, form, and gestalt. Wherever we are, it is space's purpose to make room for our actions, whereas built form ought to express the character of the place relative to the life that takes place. We use the word "gestalt" to denote motifs that identify place, and that we recognize and recall. When Heidegger says that a neighborhood "is placed under the expanse of the sky," this means that any place comprises a sky as well, and that building conjoins this with the chthonic environment. Visualization of a place can occur in two ways: either in representing the given in a corresponding architecture, or in complementing the given by adding that which the environment lacks. The two methods always operate together, but we can see in the foregoing that the South is less in need of complement than the unfinished North.[29] Our task is thus to investigate in what manner the Nordic environment has been visualized in Nordic architecture.

Heddal Stave Church, Norway

We have suggested that northern space is primarily a clearing rather than a comprehensive Euclidean whole. A clearing, however, presupposed a context within which it opens, and this we have characterized as a space of moods. This implies that northern space is not geometric but topological. The Nordic settlement has, therefore, a less precise form than in the South. That which is lacking of figural quality is compensated for by varied repetition of related forms, which operate as links in a process of growth. While open repetition manifests the Nordic environment as given, the clearing complements that which is missing; thus the whole becomes a place for dwelling.

Nordic built form is also founded in a combination of representation and complementation. In this manner, nature's web is manifest in anti-plastic skeleton construction and ornament. The line is its primary expressive element, which takes the form of half-timbered and stave construction. Log-coursing is another form of the web, even though its aim is the creation of a cavelike interior that corresponds to exterior clearing. In Norway when such a space is decorated with "rose painting," traditional eighteenth-century floral decoration, it is to enable summer to survive the winter, that is, to complement a lack. In the North, stone is employed only exceptionally, and not plastically, but rather as rustication that recalls a scree.[30]

Olav Hansson, rosepainted interior, Norway

It follows that the Nordic gestalt lacks the rounded-thing quality of the South's "wholeness." Thus gable and spire replace arcade and cupola.

Stockholm

Helsinki

Copenhagen

Gables and spires are, in their essence, anticlassical; in fact, Italian has no word for "gable." It is characteristic of the northern gestalt that it is often decomposed, such that its outline becomes compound and mobile. In general, the wholes of Nordic architecture seem incomplete, in the state of becoming.

The history of Nordic architecture illustrates these basic traits and proves that the Nordic art of building truly exists. One might even say that the domestic emerges more strongly in the North than in many other cultural areas, perhaps due to its peripheral position with respect to Europe. Nordic architecture has thus come to play a pioneering role in the development of the "new regionalism" of the postwar years.[31] The need for an architecture rooted in place can be seen as a reaction against the international style that dominated the interwar years and contributed to making our surrounding increasingly characterless and anonymous. It is therefore highly relevant to attain a deeper understanding of Nordic architecture.

In the foregoing, we have concentrated on the North-South relation and passed over the lands that lie between—that is, those countries that to differing degrees represent a synthesis of Nordic and classic traits. France offers an especially clear example of this symbiosis, perhaps because it is the only European country that borders both the Mediterranean and the North Sea. To be sure, Gothic is considered the Nordic style par excellence, but though it employs both the web and the line of force, it is inconceivable without the classic ratio.[32] In Germany, the Nordic is more directly present, but German expressionism also reflects a desire to step consciously forward in a southern way. The baroque, however, succeeded in producing a convincing synthesis of Nordic movement and classic order.[33] Finally, it must be mentioned that the English sought to conjoin Nordic mood and classic character in the "sublime."

In general, we may say that anticlassic Nordic forms presuppose the classic. Classicism is, essentially, the basic language against which all local and temporal forms must be measured, for in spite of its regional origins, the South's understanding of nature and humankind has a fundamental, general value. In Southern sun-space, the archetypal emerges, while in northern darkness it shows itself only in glimpses. Nordic artists have, therefore, always traveled to the South to learn composition—that is, to acquire the tools that ease the capture and presentation of the northern world's unfathomable web. But we should not forget that the goal is to manifest this world, not to transplant the classic. The term *anticlassic,* then, does not imply the abolition of the classic but its transformation in accordance with the Nordic environment. We have suggested how this may occur, with the words *dematerialization* and *fragmentation,* and to these we may add *deformation* and *metamorphosis.* In Nordic architecture, column and pilaster extend beyond all human proportion; frontispiece break and detail are combined in bizarre and meaningless ways.[34] Nonetheless, they resound with classicism, as that which is contradicted.

J. S. Sirén, apartments in Oulu, Finland

Porvoo Cathedral, Finland

Although it is not our aim to account for the conjunction of the Nordic and classic in the intermediate lands, it is necessary to comment on the North's relation to its more immediate neighbors. In addition to the North-South contrast, there is a significant East-West relation, and this is due to both the qualitative nature of the cardinal directions and the division of the North into eastern and western regions. Even though Sweden and Norway form a peninsula, they turn their backs to each other. This is a result not only of the mountain range that forms their common border but of the fact that, for the most part, communication was earlier conducted by sea. Norway, therefore, belongs to the lands that surround the North Sea, while Sweden and Finland are bound to those around the Baltic Sea. Thus, a major publication on Sweden begins by characterizing it as Baltic, whereas Norway is considered Atlantic. Furthermore, it declares: "The Åland Sea and the Gulf of Bothnia have rather joined than divided us from Finland."[35] Denmark's role as a middle link must likewise be emphasized, as it was the cause of Copenhagen's important historical presence. Finally, we may mention the borderless passage between the Russian and Finnish forests.

The Nordic environment is to a great degree marked by this East-West relation and by the unequal contact with the Continent. When, for example, one travels from Oslo to Stockholm, one notices the appearance of an eastern character not far into Sweden. This is a result of both landscape and building and, above all, another mood. In Finland, the eastern tinge is even stronger, and one realizes that this Baltic peculiarity is due to a meeting of different characters; from the east, the south, and the west, they are gathered around the Baltic Sea to form a special variant of the Nordic. This particular "species" is as yet little understood, even though the Swedish art historian Johnny Roosval defined already in 1923 "the Baltic-Nordic art region."[36] Within this encompassing region, we can detect other, more specific meeting places, such as Gotland and Skåne; these regions support the contention that in the past the sea united rather than divided. Denmark's connection to northern Germany and Holland is clear; these cultural regions bear a family likeness. Sweden's relation to northeastern middle Europe is less obvious, but common traits are evident in their building traditions. Even in Norway an eastern manner prevails from Trondheim and northward, whereas the southern areas show the signs of Danish influence.

In what does the eastern character we speak of consist? The East-West axis is of another sort than the North-South contrast in that it coincides with the sun's path rather than traversing and leaving it. Here, accordingly, it is not an issue of explanation versus concealment, but of beginning and end. In the East, that which will attain full form in the South is born; in the West, it will die. And so appears the eastern European landscape; as endless extension, it does not consist of definite places, even though earth and water are divided. Indeed, in the East, even primal forces slumber. In the West, conversely, all sinks into the sea. The North, therefore, plays a

R. Pietilä, Otaniemi, Finland

V. Lauritzen, transit hall, Kastrup Airport, Denmark

particular role among the cardinal points; here, we speak not of origin, end, and explanation but of a counterpole to the complete world of the South. In the North, primal forces govern, even though humans have been able in some degree to tame them, aided by southern enlightenment. When we turn to the East, we see this contrast transformed into veiled latency, expressed neither as web nor as eidetic gestalt but as a sort of picturesque suggestion of something that requires sun-space to attain its own identity.[37] When this expression encounters the Nordic, the forces are obscured by softer motifs that overlay or break through the basic Nordic form; it is this symbiosis that characterizes the Baltic.

Thus our provisional answer to the question of what identifies the Nordic world ends with a sketch of Europe's "mythic geography."[38] This may seem speculative and oversimplified, but the structure we have sought to describe is based on century-old recognitions of real qualitative differences. In this sense, it is as true as modern natural science; only its aim is different. We are not concerned with defining measurable quantities but with grasping that with which we as humans identify, which thus constitutes the foundation of our "life-world." Only in this manner can we draw closer to the Nordic—as essence, and mode of expression.

Our search for the Nordic may perhaps seem a nostalgic reaction to our times' increasing dilution of qualitative difference. Granted, but that is precisely why nostalgia has become imperative—not as a desire to turn back, however, but as a need to preserve the given through new interpretation. We may call this process "creative conservation," and find confirmation for the approach in the eco-crisis. We may add that new interpretations can indeed be found, and these corroborate that the Nordic is still a reality. Even today, the North is different; one feels this already upon arrival at Copenhagen's Kastrup airport. In Vilhelm Lauritzen's large hall, the experience of another world is immediate. In this space, intimate and warm despite its dimensions, one meets the domestic. For the traveling Scandinavian, Kastrup signifies homecoming. The word *home,* as we have suggested, is a key to the Nordic. In the North, life does not ensue on the piazza but in the home, and this entails that intimacy and warmth are more important than representative grandeur. At Kastrup, these qualities are present thanks to dimensioning, use of materials, and lighting. Although the hall is modern, it is simultaneously Danish and Nordic. Thus, the North is something more than just a cardinal point, even in this space age.

When we continue our journey through the Nordic lands, the world we have sought to present in a preliminary, general way discloses itself. For the visitor who has learned to perceive the spirit of place, the journey can be a revelation both rich and unfathomable, even overwhelmingly new. And perhaps this revelation can induce the understanding that nature, life, and architecture are insolubly bound.

Plate 1. Porvoo, Finland

Plate 2. *Light*. Skorve i Flatdal, Norway

Plate 3. N. Astrup, *St. Hans's Day Bonfire*

Plate 4. H. Sohlberg, *Winternight in Rondane*

Plate 5. H. Sohlberg, *Flowering Meadow in the North*

Plate 6. A. Edelfeldt, *Kaukola Ridge at Sunset*

Plate 7. Prince Eugen, *The Cloud*

Plate 10. Sognefjord, Norway

Plate 8. Olav Hansson, rosepainted interior, Norway

Plate 9. Heddal Stave Church, Norway

Plate 11. Osvika, Skåtøy, Norway

Plate 12. Danish clouds

Plate 13. Danish landscape

Plate 14. Liselund, Møn, Denmark

Plate 15. House in Strängnäs, Sweden

Plate 16. Finnish Landscape (Nyland)

Plate 17. Half-timbered house, Stevns Pond, Møn,
Denmark

Plate 18. "The wharf" in Bergen

Plate 19. Street in Trondheim

Plate 20. Lomen Stave Church, Norway

Plate 21. Petäjavesi Church, Finland

Plate 22. Härkeberga Church, Uppland, Sweden,
exterior

Plate 23. Härkeberga Church, Uppland, Sweden,
interior

Plate 24. Hjartdal Church, Telemark, Norway

Plate 25. C. Larson, "Lilla Hyttnäs," Sundborn,

Plate 26. C. Larson, "Lilla Hyttnäs," Sundborn, Sweden

Plate 27. L. I. Wahlman, "Tallom," near Stockholm

Plate 28. Flakstad, Lofoten, Norway

Plate 29. L. Backer, Skansen Resturant, Oslo

Plate 30. R. Erskine, project for a subarctic settlement

Plate 31. H. Sohlberg, motif from Røros, Norway

Prince Eugen, *The Forest*

The map is one of our most important resources for the understanding of place. It informs us about the naturally given places that may make room for human life as well as the settlement's answer to its natural environs through localization and distribution. This is seen not only in the configurations that the map renders in contour and relief but also in the names that it bears. All the names on a map denote places, the naturally given or the constructed. The naturally given have names because we have acknowledged them as identities, for only that which is can be named. Constructed place, too, is named, since it requires a corresponding stability in order to fulfill its mission.

We have designated the identity of place as *genius loci* and have maintained that built place, the settlement, has as its mission to make visible that which is given. The settlement and the buildings that compose it do not exist in isolation but as elements of a context that they represent and complement. The map shows how this occurs as spatial organization, and when supplemented by images of those forms that rise in space, we can truly sense what an environment is like. It is thus hardly accidental that old city atlases as a rule present place as plan and prospect; similarly architecture is documented in plan and elevation. The plan (the map) shows how space is distributed between walls, while the elevation gives the whole presence as built form. When these two aspects are combined in a perspective that represents the thing's contour, we can recognize its gestalt or figural quality.[1]

In order to better understand the role of the North in its larger context, we need only glance at a map of Europe. It tells us much we need to know concerning the identities and reciprocal relations of countries and cultural regions. Above all, it shows how well-defined the large nations of western, middle, and southern Europe are, and how the Continent as a whole emerges from the east and ends in the west, while its forms disperse toward the north. The map also shows that Europe's center is in the Alps. From this mountain range flow Europe's great rivers in all directions, and that which had its source in a common mount flowers in those cultural regions where this movement from the center falls to rest. These regions bear reminders of the source and dispatch messages back to the origin.

Architecture discloses this process. In Ticino, classic form from the *light-saturated* South encounters a stronger world, losing its clement plasticity. The anthropomorphic column approaches the Nordic line of force, and the wall obtains archaic weight. In the Swiss midlands, the half-timbered house's Nordic web conjoins the earthbound; under the enormous roof of the Bernese Oberland farmhouse, the half-timber lines emerge like ripples on a more elemental form. The West's Gothic skeleton acquires another substance in this Swiss mountain world, losing much of its French rationalism. The last offshoots of the Slavic East appear finally in baroque onion domes, completing the movement back to the common center. In this manner, Europe's horizontal axes find a symbolic vertical at their crossing.

2

The Natural

Danish clouds

Danish landscape

The Nordic lands lie at the periphery of this larger picture.[2] Denmark is linked to the Continent, but when we enter from the extensive northern German plains, the landscape is transformed: extension is fragmented and the scale becomes more intimate. The Danish national song's refrain, "meanders in hill and dale," suggests this transformation. But at the same time, strangely, all becomes larger. A ridge need not rise greatly to provide view; when nothing obstructs the glance, the eye travels far and free. Small and intimate Denmark is thus a "large" country. This double character is aptly demonstrated in its contour, which because of its five hundred islands and innumerable bays forms a varied and kinetic whole. Where the coast is steep, it seems like an edge bounding open land and creating place as peninsula and island. What lies within the contour is also filled with surprises, though dramatic effects are few and far between in a land where the highest elevation is a mere 550 feet above sea level. Nonetheless, Denmark is known for its

Liselund, Møn, Denmark

hills and varied views. Innumerable intimate places are formed simultaneously within the undulatory relief. Here, one comes near to things; the land's
intimate scale facilitates identification and participation. The Danes' own
descriptions are characteristic and rich in details of grass, flowers, and
trees—and fragrance and sound, for that matter. "One sees blue water
through the beech leaves and high grass, through fine swaying nettles and
polychrome flowers."[3] Nearness is thus this land's most immediate quality.
But what we grasp, however, is not discrete characters but fluid nuance, in
an interplay throughout a mobile space of mood.

Cliffs at Møn, Denmark

      This earthly realm of nuance is gathered under the heavens, which,
as in all flat countries, achieve power and majesty. But it is also Nordic—
that is, it is not a blue vault of sky but the "theater" of the clouds. Thus
weather, as in all Nordic lands, defines the environment: "The most beautiful
is perhaps the view over the land in storm, with driving clouds and distant
showers, sweeping across the plains." "And finally the hours of the day ac-
company an uninterrupted transformation. This view one thinks one knows
so well in afternoon's mild light, is quite another by full moon, and again
new, at sunrise."[4]

      Since Denmark is restricted in size, all its effects are subdued, and
the differences among its parts are less marked than in the other Nordic
countries. The North-South tension is essentially absent, but the East-West
relation plays a certain role. Thus Jutland turns its back to the North Sea
with a relatively desolate, windblown coast. Toward the east, conversely, the
land is fertile and idyllic; this character, with certain differences in nuance,
is typical of the insular region centered in Zeeland. Here, the land flattens;
space enlarges and attains new power. The plains of Skåne, through centuries

Map of Scandinavia

Danish house beneath trees

Kundby Church, Zealand, Denmark

Liselund, Møn, Denmark

Danish territory, continue this image and reinforce Zeeland's central position. Øresund was thus the major artery of the country, and here Copenhagen developed. The legendary beech forest along the sound greeted the visitor with a beautiful impression of Europe's "most charming and well-maintained country."[5] It is, indeed, a charming country, but also an ordered and reasonable one.

How can architecture maintain and represent this Danish environment? As elsewhere, localization of settlement is determined by the naturally given place. The creations of the community thereby express the use of the land: harbor, ford, ferry dock. The landscape's fragmented continuum requires further that built areas be concentrated. We may say, then, that the Danish clearing is a closed yard; though this is not to say that it is isolated from its surroundings. The Danish settlement creates, rather, a soft passage toward the open land through the use of gardens and vegetation. Nearness to nature is thus a characteristic quality. This is demonstrated in the manner in which building adapts topographic movement and rhythm, presupposing small, low units: earth-hugging, one-story houses with thatched roofs. Buildings lie in the hollows, under the trees, rather than between them. And when trunks and branches find echo in the lines of half-timbered construction, the unity of natural and the artificial is completed. The Danish farmyard unites these qualities in a topologically closed *firlænge* (literally, four-winged, or courtyard farm) of simple volumes with repetitive wall structure.

Against these down-to-earth dwellings, the churches stand in contrast. Hilltops have since ancient times been holy ground, and Denmark has more than seventy thousand burial mounds, some crowned with dolmens, from which the dead might gaze out over the land. Since the Middle Ages, the church has usurped the role of the mound as center in the landscape, but it never dominates. Its effect is subdued by the use of stepped gables and additively built-up towers, and the interior's low vaults and murals echo the tree stand's leafy rooms. The Danish churchyard maintains and visualizes the structure of the land; in low, well-clipped hedges it reifies the fragmented continuum as geometric order, and the splendor of flowers brings the whole to life.

Danish architecture, past and present, has given poetic expression to its environment. At the renowned country estate Liselund on the island of Møn (1792–95), the Danish hill and dale has become romantic, expressive: soft slopes, splendid stands of beech, reflecting pools. The house proper is a synthesis of palace and farmhouse, symmetrical in disposition, classical in detail, grouped under a thatched roof. The interior is ordered along an axis that runs from an intimate dining room toward the land without; here, indeed, all is near. Jørn Utzon's church at Bagsvaerd near Copenhagen (1973–76) offers a more recent example of how a given environment can still be validly interpreted. Here we can detect the land's repetitive order, the

J. Utzon, Bagsværd Church, near Copenhagen

restrained vertical motion in the stepped outerwalls, and the Danish sky in the undulate vaulting that captures light's transient nuances.[6]

This description of the Danish environment may seem to stand in contrast to the general characteristics of the Nordic. Danish space is certainly a true mood space—its horizontal extension topologically continuous rather than classically axial—but, concurrently, the classic impress is more conspicuous here than elsewhere in the North. A small country of meager resources requires a certain order in cultivation and building; thus Danish architecture is simultaneously idyllic and precise. But Danish classicism lacks southern plasticity and hence represents the Nordic contradiction. Above all, Denmark distinguishes itself in that the primal forces are tamed: the troll has become nymph and elf. It is no accident that its national symbol has become the little mermaid.

A text of 1777 describes Norway as one enormous rock, riven with valleys.[7] The image is accurate, for there is scarcely another country united to such a degree by mountains. The condition may be seen as an inversion of the Swiss Alps: whereas the Alps are a center that erupts within its surroundings, the

Flatdal, Telemark, Norway

Osvika, Skåtøy, Norway   Sognefjord, Norway

Norwegian mountain is a compact mass stretching out from above, dispersing itself westward as precipice and skerry, eastward in progressively smaller fragments. This fragmentation occurs primarily in Sweden and continues through Åland into Finland. In Norway, the mountain mass still coheres, and therefore the valley emerges as rift. The fjords in the west are likewise but waterfilled. In this manner, Norwegian spatial structure is as different from the Danish as is possible. Here, one lives not in an extensive, open environment but between high walls; and although Norway is larger and more vigorous than its southern sister, it seems smaller because it lacks prospect. It is only when one is on top of the mountains that prospect becomes panorama, and hence it is the Norwegian dream to reach "over the high mountains."[8] But it is down in the valley that everyday life takes place, and the Norwegian is thus *døl* (dalesman), a word absent from most other tongues.

This general characteristic does not imply that Norway is an undiversified country. On the contrary, its regions are more varied than in most lands, and it is noteworthy that these regions are named for cardinal directions: Østland, Sørland, Vestland, Nordland—that is, the lands to the east, south, west, and north. Only two regions escape this classification, Trøndelag and Finnmark, evidently because they play a special role within the whole. Each of these regions has a distinct character: Østland is a region of valleys and deep woods; Sørland, by Norwegian standards, a smiling stretch of coastline, of harbors, and skerries; Vestland, the dramatic region of narrow fjords, where mountain meets the sea; while Nordland combines fjord, mountain, and coastline in a landscape where untamed forces govern.[9] If one pictures this structure, it becomes clear that Trøndelag forms the center of this aggregate; here, the fjord broadens, in surprise and variation. The effect is reinforced by Trondheim's northward orientation: one has one's back to the sun, looking out over the broad fjord. Insofar as it is possible so far north, light suffuses space, and the surroundings appear calm. These features contributed to making Nidaros (Trondheim) Norway's center in the Middle Ages.[10]

When we return to the cardinal regions from their common center, their deeper meanings emerge. The valleys of Østland can be seen as they are, leading each in its own way into the land, toward the source. It is not possible here to examine each valley individually, but we shall say a few words about Telemark, which more than any other region is known as the Norwegian folktale landscape. Its name is significant, referring not to a single valley but to a *mark* (field); in any case, it is an area of manifold dales, forming an unsurveyable whole. On a map of southern Norway from 1635, both coastline and valleys are delineated, but Telemark is shown as a large white patch.[11] The topography of this area was evidently too complex, and the cartographer was forced to give up. Even today, it is difficult to form a total image of this region: ridge after ridge, fuzzy hills and mountains, rugged cliffs, rocks covered by moss; new valleys and hidden cirques appear constantly, a tangle of spatial entities always leading farther. But some of these places conjoin the troll-like with the idyllic and reveal the benign side of primal force.[12] The Norwegian writer Terjei Vesaas, from Vinje in Telemark, describes it thus:

> Unrest. And searching for rest. It is certainly the terrain, the landscape itself, which must be sought as cause for the uneven temperament that is our distinguishing feature. Telemark encompasses all too many unlike landscapes. A confusion of valleys. Bare rockfaces and empty plateaus. Protracted forests. And water in all forms. Naked, frozen, and windblown little farms in the mountains. Warm and flourishing, rich farms under a friendly sky in the lowlands. Wild and pleasant, ugly and beautiful; this awaits he who would dissect Telemark.[13]

The Norwegian valley shows that our being in space is determined by a tension of above and below. In valleys, we are below; this is our place of dwelling, where we create the order supporting our existence. Here, people are at home, and animals are safe. Here, place is an understood world, even in threatening weather. But in Norway, this order is, from nature's side, only a rift in the unknown. Mountains loom above, the enormous stone uniting the land. And when we ascend, we are calmed by a freedom that is different from the valley's safety, because on the top we are exposed. Here, "up in the weather," forces are unleashed as in a storm, and we understand that the "panorama" is a fragile condition.[14]

Vestvågøy, Lofoten, Norway

Trondheim, Norway

Mølster Tun, Voss, Norway

Heddal Stave Church, Norway

Flakstad, Lofoten, Norway

In Østland, the difference between above and below is considerable, if not so great as in central Europe; and even though the mountains above the fjords of Vestland loom, they are distant. But if we travel northward, the mountains progressively encroach. The belt of farming, forest, and settlement shrinks until in north Norway it is but a narrow strip along the sea. Here, in Lofoten, high mountain and sea are conjunctive. Suddenly, the sky is near, not as redemptive quietude but as savagery, amplified by peaked mountains and spiked contours, by their naked faces, marked by crevices and scree and seemingly a cascade of boulders. As such, the mountains violently rise and simultaneously rage down. Wild and unyielding, they resist classification, indeed seem to have been halted midway through Creation. Here, earth and sky are joined, the eye finds no rest, and the Nordic way becomes identical with nature itself. Instability consists as well of ever-changing weather: haze and rain, hail and snow, clouds unceasingly in motion, closing and opening while light penetrates, then disappears. A world of eternal motion that, however, remains the same.

> The air sparkled with moisture and sunlight. In unforgettable silver-white rows, the cumulonimbus came roving in from over the sea, casting light and shadow alternately against my eye, over me and around me they were, and went past, past, overturning against the Vega mountains, its sharp peaks met them like black knife thrusts, tore apart, rent to pieces, and the cloud bank became a solitary white shadow, fleeing over the pass.[15]

Magnus Poulsson, sketch

Such is the forceful expression of the Norwegian environment of the far North, and though Norwegian architecture developed farther south, it is northern Norway that reveals its deepest meaning.

How, then, can architecture represent and maintain this Norwegian world? How can building be concurrently wild and safe; how can it provide a foothold in an environment constantly in motion? Again, if we examine spatiality, we can ascertain that in Norway a clear resonance exists between landscape-type and settlement-form. In this extensive land of scattered inhabitants, it is the *gård* (yard, farm compound) rather than the village that is fundamental, and earlier it assumed the role of town.[16] The Norwegian term *tun* demonstrates this: it is cognate with "town" and the German "Zaun." Hence the gård is a delimited place in the natural surroundings, in its way a clearing. But a tun may be organized in several manners, three of which are commonly found in Norway: the cluster, the row, and the more or less closed rectangle. These correspond, in principle, to village and town formations that are in evidence in other countries, and they also represent a manifestation of the "gestalt laws."[17] That is to say, these manners of organization belong to a common language that ought to be used in resonance with the given place. This is exactly what occurs in Norway. The cluster tun

J. Rønjom, "Loft," Kultan, Åmotsdal, Norway

Swedish landscape with knolls

developed in Vestland, where narrow, irregular sites demand a free disposition of the buildings. The row tun is used, on the other hand, in narrow, extended valleys, in evidence in the purest form in Setesdal, whereas the closed rectangle shows up in Trøndelag, indicative of that landscape's comprehensive quality.[18] As clearing and delimitation, the tun complements naturally given place, whereas the choice of type represents given space. Therefore, the tun is, in a very real sense, a home where nature is explained.

But the Norwegian place is above all determined by the tension of above and below; here, things exist not in harmonic presence within comprehensive space but instead participate in the environmental interplay of forces. To reveal and maintain this in building requires forms that simultaneously possess the safety of home and express the indefinite and savage environment. The next chapter shows how this problem was solved with the combination of stave and log construction, the two methods that form the basis of Norwegian wooden architecture. Now we shall only suggest how architectonic form can be simultaneously heavy and light, and embody thereby the tension of below and above. In the "loft" at Kultan in Åmotsdal (c. 1790), builder Jarand Rønjom employed timbers laid horizontally to create a secure "cave of wood," while he united the timber ends to form a springy, rising curve. The result is a building that both rests and ascends, thus embodying the Norwegian relation of earth and sky. Here, forms speak the language of the land.

Finally, we must ask how architecture can maintain Norwegian light. We have described the transient quality of light in the North and have asserted that only on winter nights is the sky large and unified, filled with "dark light." The stave church reifies this light. In its interior, heavenward structural masts are lost in the reaches of upper darkness, where small peep-

Siljan, Dalarne, Sweden

Mälaren Lake near Sigtuna, Sweden

Strägnäs, street with cathedral, Sweden

holes illuminate like stars. Thus can darkness illuminate and disclose the deepest significances of the midnight world. Shifting summer light does not achieve this but is instead kept in the rose-painted cottage, where life may survive the winter. But there is also another possible explanation of Norwegian nature. The small wooden church at Flakstad in Lofoten (1780) mimics no mountain; it stands as simple volume in complement to savage nature. Its onion spire is the only element rising in space; its tense curve is reminiscent of Rønjom's timber wall, at the same time as it recalls a larger context. Thus the church becomes a focus that gathers nature as place.

In this century, it has not been easy for architects to find expression of the Norwegian environment. A time that sets functionalism as a goal appears to preclude nature's interplay, but an architecture that cannot manifest the unity of life and place falls short and cannot satisfy the need for home. As a result, some have begun to again interpret the Norwegian environs as built form. Magnus Poulsson's sketches reveal this search—a search toward the representation of nature's tensions and play of forces.

From the west, the mountainous ground advances over the border into Sweden; the farther east, the more fragmented its mass becomes. Thus Svealand's topography appears as an inversion of the Norwegian. Whereas Norway is a single enormous rock, split with crevices, mid-Sweden is a large and continuous land filled with mountainous remainders: this is the landscape that has determined the Swedish identity, in the natural and the constructed. Svealand is, indeed, Sweden; facing east, it surrounds Lake Mälar, a sort of Swedish counterpart to the west-oriented Trøndelag. Here again, we are midland; here again, water is the gathering element. But here, the Baltic is imminent, for while Trondheim Fjord is Atlantic, Lake Mälar is a continuation of the Baltic Sea, and where sea and lake converge, we find Stockholm.[19] Svealand thus has a unique position, and as an inland region in direct contact with the sea, it was predetermined to be Sweden's heartland. "[I]t is indisputable that the Swedish realm's oldest nucleus lay in the cultivated plains around the Mälar."[20] And due to Lake Mälar's central position, division by cardinal directions was natural: Uppland in the north, Västmanland in the west, Södermanland to the south, and eastward we are led through skerries toward the Baltic Sea. The lake itself is subdivided like the coast and the surrounding land. Innumerable islands and bays mark Svealand and result in a character woven of water and land that "makes the Swedes as capable with sail and oar as with rein and plow."[21] It is only toward Uppsala that the landscape begins to even, becoming a landscape of larger features and making it the region's "center of gravity." Sea contact was established in Sigtuna through a branch of Lake Mälar; as Svealand's first bishopric, the town played an important role until it was sacked by Estonians in 1181. This event is central to understanding why Stockholm was founded in the mid-1200s as a lock on Lake Mälar and Svealand's fortified harbor.

Västerås Cathedral, vaulting, Sweden

C. Nyrén, Gottsunda Church near Uppsala, Sweden

Finnish landscape (Nyland)

House in Strängnäs, Sweden

Swedish sky

In our discussion, the topography of the region is of greatest import. We have suggested that Svealand appears as a weave of water and land, where a flat continuum forms a ground for innumerable hills and knolls—in Swedish, *kullar*. The land is fertile, and by Nordic standards "smiling," but it is very different from the Danish countryside. In Svealand, it is the kullar that afford a hold for vegetation and building, while the interstices are cultivated. In this manner, the cultivated field provides a continuous ground for applied, quasi-figurative elements. And though the soil is fertile, it is thin, and the trees are relatively low. The scale, therefore, is marked by small dimensions and creates a sense of extension.

Surrounding Sweden's midregion we can find several characteristic regions, and again, the cardinal points provide the general structure. Toward the north we find the enormous Norrland, encompassing many landscapes; these have in common larger land features, with regard to both topography and woodland. And though a kinship with Norway's Østland exists, the sense of space is different; it is only at the immediate border to Norway that Sweden gains a mountainous character. Between Svealand and Norrland is Dalarne, a region rich in agriculture and monuments, which deserves the denomination "cultural land."[22] South of Svealand lies Sweden's second principle area, Götaland, divided east-west by Lake Vättern. The influence of Denmark and the Continent was assimilated earliest and strongest in Götaland, which was moreover Christianized earlier than Svealand. Consequently, Götaland's Swedish character is somewhat less marked. It is also important to note that it is mainly an inland region, where contact with the sea is of secondary importance.[23] Toward the south, historic Sweden ends in the rocky and infecund Småland (Small land). As the name implies, this region lies outside the large and fertile landscapes just described. Småland is a highland (although its highest point lies only 1100 feet above sea level), and rivers flow from here in all directions. Thus it acts as a natural boundary to Skåne, the southwestern coastal region that seems a continuation of the Danish islands.

Sweden is one of Europe's largest countries, comprising numerous distinct regions. As a result, it stands in contrast to uniform Denmark, but also to Norway, where differences are more deeply impressed by its dramatic nature. For despite regional differences, Sweden appears a continuous land, albeit rich in varied detail. This varied continuum is especially characteristic of Svealand, where Sweden's identity is most evident. If we designate Denmark's mood as a play of nuance, and Norway's as a drama of contrasts, then Sweden's appears as a manifold of memories. Here, we are reminded of natural forces rather than experiencing them directly; here, we are reminded of environmental characters such as Norway's mountain world in the kullar, Finland's wilderness in Norrland's forests, and Denmark's undulating ground in the friendly Skåne. The map shows us that this is natural, since Sweden is at the center of the Nordic world, surrounded by western, southern, and eastern areas.

How, then, is Sweden's compound nature realized as architecture? The answer is through an eclectic combination of those characters that are gathered by the land itself.[24] Such, then, is Swedish architecture; upon general basic forms emerge three distinct memories: west European, north German, and Baltic. A faceted and exciting image arises, wherein known characters appear in new guise, and wherein many may find support for personal identification. But the basic forms, as such, are they not Swedish? Of course, a basic form is never exclusively locally conditioned but represents a special synthesis of basic possibilities, and because it is synthetic, it feels immediately domestic. Any culture, however, necessarily comprises numerous basic forms that share common traits. The typical forms of Swedish architecture, for instance, always become manifest as a continuous ground on which detail appears; this characteristic trait parallels the land itself. The forms are, as a rule, down-to-earth, indeed squat, though detail may be lively enough. A characteristic basic Swedish form is the heavy, low tower, generally round, but also square in connection with churches, which culminates in elaborate upper terminations. Another is the "broken gable," formed like an unhipped mansard roof. This roof form, known as *gambrel*, became immigrant Swedes's hallmark in America.[25] Like the squat tower, it is a form that stresses the closed volume.

Since Sweden's regions do not exhibit the degree of spatial variety found in Norway, its types of tun likewise are not so diverse. The rectangular tun is customary in more or less closed versions; and not surprisingly, the wholly closed *firlænge* is common in Skåne.[26] In Norrland, a rectangular tun that recalls the Norwegian Trønderlag tun is common. In general, architectonic space is related to natural space; as clearing, it must necessarily adapt to the given structure of the surroundings. The lack of type variation is compensated by the modes of building, which differ with latitude, from the Danish *sleppvegg* (hewn horizontal panels that are slipped down in grooves between vertical supports) and half-timber construction in Skåne to log construction in the north. Mid-Sweden is characterized by the locklistpanel (vertical clapboard), early in use. But regardless of the mode of building, the houses are low and earth hugging and lack Norwegian timber architecture's tensive rising.

Light is also a significant environmental factor in Sweden, but again its difference from the Danish or Norwegian is conspicuous. For while Danish light is primarily pure light from the sky, and Norwegian light appears to be in a space delimited by walls, the Swedish light seems filtered, recalling the light qualities of both neighbor lands and betokening the cleft Finnish light. Vesterås Cathedral visualizes the mobile grey-white sky of the North in an unparalleled manner, at the same time as the space becomes a "cave." The medieval star-vaults are relatively low, with heavy ribs and deepset webs decorated with floral motifs in pastel tones, with the effect that the sky is represented as a "happy Eden."

Finnish lake

Finnish forest

Raahe Square, Finland

Contemporary Swedish architecture has been successful in translating its environs into built form. As we shall see later, Ragnar Östberg, Carl Westman, and Gunnar Asplund are Swedish architects in the true sense of the word, in that they achieve new interpretations of the interplay of elemental form and eclectic application. Recently, Carl Nyrén has joined their ranks. His church at Gottsunda near Uppsala (1980) combines in this way a series of "known" motifs into a Swedish whole. Since eclecticism has again become present, Swedish architecture is of great interest; this fact is evidenced by monographs on architects that modernism forgot.[27]

In order to understand Finland's topography, one should fly from Stockholm to Helsinki in winter. Then one can see how Svealand's kullar continue through the Åland islands to the other shore of the Gulf of Bothnia. Early winter covers all horizontal surfaces with snow, while the tree-clad hills emerge bare and dark. Innumerable and various in size, the hills seem a perpetuation of the island-skerries; none are high, and the land extends toward the horizon. Farther on, they cluster somewhat, and lakes proliferate and enlarge. The whole forms a labyrinthine web, as different from Norway as possible, where water belongs to the structure of the valleys. Finland possesses no valley, its midland no plain. Here, the land is a topological continuum, without beginning and without end. And while water and land are divided, they are nonetheless interwoven. In principle, all of Finland is so constituted, but this structure is most evident in the interior zone, Hämenlääni (Tavastland), and eastward toward Karelia. A range of low ridges gives this region a certain definition with respect to the "Swedish" coast in the southwest, while on the west coast lies (Österbotten), a region of fertile plains.

Finnish forest (Vitträsk)

The regional differences are strengthened by vegetation: deciduous forests line coastal areas and coniferous trees dominate inland. These are primarily tall, thin pines, and coupled with a terrain that lacks great rise, they produce a landscape of endless uniform extension. Seventy percent of Finland is heavily forested, but stone is nonetheless omnipresent.[28] The land is less fecund than in Sweden; the granite ground acts as a continuous fundament for that which occurs in space. The terrain is often swampy, however. It is no accident that the *Kalevala's* trial of strength between Väinämöinen and Joukahainen ends with the latter sinking into the mire. Thus the Finnish land is simultaneously firm basis and bottomless abyss. This is an essential precondition for the Finns' understanding of the earth. Northward, the land flattens, the sense of endlessness culminates, and in Oulun Lääni trees are fewer, appearing on a sandy ground that is often covered by grey-green moss. Here, we do not go *into* the forest as in Norway, but rather *out* in it. As such, a new airiness is present, unlike the midlands' darker and more closed character. This airiness is emphasized by the birch tree's linear presence, embodying the cleft light.

Finland does not comprise regional character as distinct as Norway, or Sweden for that matter. It is far more uniform and, in that sense, akin to Denmark, but with essential environmental differences. Whereas Denmark is soft and smiling, Finland is hard and infecund. Nonetheless, its nature is hardly forbidding. The forest is certainly uniform, but the presence of water forms comfortable oases. The general uniformity is a mode of the unfinished; in Finland, neither form, space, nor gestalt possess the same identity as in the other Nordic countries. This entails, however, that its possibilities are greater—we have heard Väinämöinen's poetic reply to the land's challenges. It also signifies that the unfinished can be seen as the original, as a source that may become something, and that this something is present in its origins. Finland is thus the most Nordic of the Nordic lands; here coexist "solemnity and unshakeable calm, and on the other hand, an unquenchable dreamer's temperament and a volcanic striving toward dramatic form. In the painters' dark and solemn palette and the sculptors' heavy plasticity, these basic Finnish qualities become apparent."[29] Finnish artists have repeatedly emphasized their dependence on nature, that is, on the mood of the environment. The Finnish word for mood, *tunnelmaa,* denotes a conjunction of expression and feeling. The mood belongs to the environment (the thing) and is absorbed by human inhabitants, who thereby "get in the mood." Thus Sibelius set this motto over his symphonic poem, *Tapiola:*

> Outstretched they stand, the North's hazy forests. Ancient, secretive, brooding in wild dreams. Within dwells the powerful god of the forest, and tree spirits weave magical enigmas in the dusk.[30]

When the unfinished is to be realized architecturally, the balance of representation and complementation becomes a pressing issue. On the one hand, it is necessary to show where one is, on the other, to supplement that which is missing. What is to be represented here is the endless, extensive space that follows a curved trajectory toward an always receding horizon, the earthly formations of stone, lying in contrast to the thin, vertical trees and the cleft light that deprives the sky of its unifying effect. What is to be supplemented is the space where life can take place, and in a land such as this, not only is a clearing necessary but also the "cave of wood."[31] In old folk houses, then, we can find interiors where the log wall continues up to form the ceiling as well, so that a closed whole results—a solution that is sometimes also found in Sweden. The wooden vaults of Finnish churches likewise express this desire for a cavelike interior; their vaults' smooth surfaces contrast with the heavy timber walls, creating a sense of sky, an effect that is found again in the stone churches' all-white interiors. And the whiteness breaks through the wall's outer skin in a Baltic way, showing up in window jambs and decorative details. But space also requires order to attain a hold in the labyrinthine environs; thus, it is hardly coincidental that the

L. Sonck, Cathedral in Tampere (Tammerfors), Finland

classical grid attained such an importance for Finnish cities. The grid represents and complements the extension of Finnish space, while the houses' low windows lead the gaze toward the ground and secure a certain intimacy.

In general, Finnish built form is simple and suits the lack of tensions and distinct gestalt qualities of the environment. Wall and roof always form a skin around a cave or, if you will, a shell around a structure. The sacred is not expressed in special forms but primarily by churches having steeper gables than houses. The need for a balance between representation and complementation emerges later in the Empire style's linear classicism, ornamented with Russian details.

The Finns, perhaps better than anyone else, have succeeded in translating their environment into a meaningful and convincing architecture. The rediscovery of original Finnish qualities toward the close of the nineteenth century, a naturalness forgotten under Swedish and Russian rule, found expression in buildings where stone and wood work together in an unparalleled manner. We will examine these works of National Romanticism more closely in chapter 6, but note here that, as a result of this work, Finland became a leading country with regard to the development of the "new regionalism."[32] It was advanced by Alvar Aalto, whose spaces, already in the interwar years, were inspired by the Finnish landscape. This Finnish quality comes to fruition in the work of Reima Pietilä, who maintains Finnish space and form, and even succeeds in creating the strong gestalt that is needed to express the Finnish environment. This pertains especially to his Kaleva church in Tampere (1959–66), whose topological plan and closely spaced verticals bespeak the land, while it simultaneously maintains the cleft light in fissures between grey-white wall sections that rise toward a darker vault. The "measure" of the space is a sculpture by Pietilä himself, which stands like a tree in the light.

R. Pietilä, Kaleva Church in Tampere, Finland

Our description of the nature and basic forms of the Nordic countries shows that the Nordic search for the natural entails an anticlassical attitude. For though the classical also has its origins in an understanding of nature, its aim was the ideal, that is, the archetypal form that could represent a standard for all simple phenomena. In the unified space of the South, where things emerge proudly with their proper identity, such an objective is natural. The incomplete and unstable world of the North, conversely, cannot be represented and complemented in this manner. Here, nature implies nearness and empathy; here, one lives with and among things, as a participant in a web of phenomena. Mood is the basis for participation, also in the sense of cause.

We have seen, however, that participation occurs in different ways. In Denmark, things are understood through nearness, and the goal is the establishment of a friendly relationship. In Norway, things are seen as effect, and the goal is to enter into a fantastic play of powers. Sweden understands things as memories, with the aim of recalling environmental qualities. In Finland, things are experienced as possibilities, and the goal is to reveal the hidden. All of these modes have their origin in the mythic geography of the North, which humans must understand through participation in order to obtain a meaningful interaction. Common to all these lands is their incompleteness, thus Nordic understanding becomes the dream of engagement, rather than the *veduta* of the South.[33] Participation entails that custom and use substitute for ideal form, and that building tradition replaces the classic concept of style, revealing thus the importance of the domestic in the North.

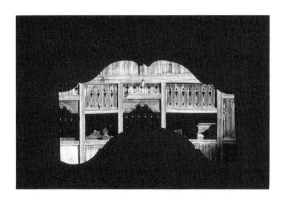

Harildstad, Heidal, Norway

The old settlement constitutes an integral part of Europe's cultural landscape. It varies with place but always appears at home in its surroundings. Indeed, it often seems that it is the settlement itself that allows the landscape to emerge as it does; reciprocally, the nature of the environs deepens the significance of the buildings. Such is the case in Mediterranean countries, and so it is in middle and northern Europe as well. The farmhouses of Berner Oberland and Schwarzwald are marvelous examples of this; Franconia's Vierkanthöfe (square farms) are, in this way, organically interwoven, and the great Hallenhäuser (hall houses) at Niedersachsen stand as a point of identification in the extensive northern German landscape.[1] We know that buildings serve practical aims, but, additionally, they belong to place and inform us where we are, what it is like to be *here*. As such, we understand how it is to be in Denmark, when facing its characteristic groups of half-timbered houses. We recognize Sweden's genius in a landscape dotted with red cottages with gambrel roofs. Norway's character arises in buildings of logs and staves, and in more recently built white farm houses and red barns. Finland's old wooden buildings spread in expression of the land's endless uniform extension. In this manner, buildings manifest the forms of life and nature and recall Heidegger's words: "The buildings bring the earth as the inhabited landscape close to man."

When we travel through a landscape or reach a place, it is the aspect of the environs that is immediately experienced; it is this aspect that tells us whether we are home or not. In other words, we identify with things according to the manner in which we perceive them, and it is evident that this perception is the result of something more than experience, for even the foreign is experienced as "something." We somehow recognize things beforehand, and thus we say of the totally new that it is "neither fish nor fowl."[2] Nevertheless, the experienced lies closer and gives a spontaneous sense of security because we know how it is. This implies that the word *aspect* connotes much more than outward appearance (eidos). Aspect always encompasses manifold meanings in that it is bound within that interplay of self and environment called *being-in-the-world*. This is not subjectivity; it is defined instead through the naturally given and that which has been passed on from earlier generations. We may call the latter *custom*. Custom is always synthetic with use; being-in-the-world requires cooperation and care. In order that customs may survive, they must manifest themselves as figures, or gestalt qualities, and thereby in an aspect.[3] These figures may appear as actions (rituals), things (clothing, objects of use), and buildings (settlement).

We have seen that the experience of an environment's aspect is the result of many factors. Light is of primary importance because it provides the surroundings with their basic mood, but topography and vegetation provide more concrete premises. And materials define the surroundings in an even more tangible way: stone and sand, tree and turf, water and snow. All of this is given, there before we "employ" the surroundings toward definite goals,

Half-timbered house, Stevns Pond, Møn, Denmark

but it is important to note that the qualities of an environment first become real when participating in a context of use, thereby partaking in the forms of life. This is the context we have in mind when we say that "life takes place." In order that life can take place, we require buildings, whose aspect or figure are determined by the customs and usages that identify life in the place. Thus *building tradition* is a meaningful term, for it renders the natural domestic by expressing human use of the given. We have maintained that this entails both representation of the preextant and complementation of the missing. In general, building tradition expresses the unity of life and place, and it is thus, above all, regional; but additionally, the regional always has a universal basis. We will call regional and domestic building *folk architecture,* because it is inextricably linked within the daily life of the people.

When today these traditions threaten to be lost, it is a symptom of the environmental crisis that is quickly gaining an upper hand; a crisis which entails that the cohesion of life and place is severed. Preservation, then, of the tradition of building is an essential aim of environmental protection. This does not imply, however, that tradition should be frozen in place, for the unity of life and place is not a static relation but a process that needs to be constantly reinterpreted, though something constant must be retained throughout variation. This "something" is the core of a building tradition.

What, then, is this core? Our brief references to Danish, Swedish, Norwegian, and Finnish traditions comprised many factors: the grouping of houses, roof formations, color, and construction. This list might be greatly enlarged to include, for example, characteristic window and entry formations, interior elements, and decoration. To get an overview and understanding it is convenient, as we saw earlier, to group these factors in the categories

"Bulverk" construction, Gotland, Sweden

space, built form, and gestalt quality. This division is not formalistic but implies instead that we take the context of use as a basis, for it is spatial organization that makes possible our orientation, while built form acts as an object for identification, and gestalt quality forms the content of our memory. The *spatial* concerns both a building's relation to its surroundings (situation), and its internal disposition (plan); *built form* is bound primarily to the use of material and technical execution (building method); *gestalt quality* is both wholes (mass, volume), and secondary elements (motifs). When space, form, and gestalt quality remain relatively stable through time and space, and thereby become building tradition, they attain typological value.

But although space, form, and gestalt quality belong together, it is far from certain that they are typically manifest with like regularity. Spatial organization may remain stable throughout large regions and for long periods, while building methods vary. A characteristic gestalt, moreover, is not necessarily interdependent with particular building methods. In this manner, certain plan configurations occur in Nordic folk architecture without a building's aspect being thereby determined. It is evident that this is a result of the continued sameness of human activity, despite variation in environmental character. Gestalt qualities can remain unchanged through generations, while detailing and articulation vary with respect to regional and temporal difference.[4] The question of what it is that remains, therefore, is not immediately answerable.

The use of the term *remains* connotes that some thing has been in the main self-same since its inception, though it may develop and vary along the way. This applies to all things organic as well as to basic architectural gestalt qualities. The history of architecture discloses that each gestalt is defined with respect to its original formation. As a whole of symbiotic parts, a gestalt has a structure, which becomes comprehensible if we research the relationships of its parts to one another. The German linguist Jost Trier, who has investigated in a series of basic studies the meaning of the more important architectural terms, states: "A word that denotes a link in a built whole cannot be considered in isolation but can only be understood within its context. Its placement within the whole defines its meaning."[5] The term *gable,* for example, stems from the gable post (forked post) that in early wooden construction supported the ridge beam at each end of a building. Its primary role led to its Old High German name *Irminsul* (universal column), that which supports all things.[6] Analogously, the ridge beam was the "celestial axis" around which the world is ordered, a conception that corresponds to the Roman cardo that runs from the North star to the Southern sun (Vitruvius).[7] Together, the fork and the ridge beam gave the house its contour, and thereby its character or gestalt quality. We call this a gable and can see that a term that originally denoted a constructive link was transposed upon a typical form that survives despite the alterations of technical execution. In Trier's terminology, a "framework-idea" (*Gerüstbegriff*) becomes a "locus-idea" (*Gegendbegriff*); that is, it becomes something that pertains to the aspect of building.[8] Such a translation from construction to gestalt is a decisive step in the development of a building tradition as an architectonic language of form.

Is it then typic form, or gestalt, that constitutes the core of building tradition? The answer is yes—but only if we acknowledge formal essence; if we understand "aspect" to mean always something more than "outward appearance." What does this entail? Trier's investigations reveal that buildings originally formed a world-image. This is well known as it applies to major components such as floor, wall, roof. Many words remind us of this, for example, "ceiling," from the Latin *caelum,* (the heavens).[9] Less well known, however, is that building method, too, had a depictive function. In general, we may say that the world was earlier comprehended as a "big house," and that the works of humans represented this structure.[10] Through detailing and articulation, it was possible to maintain the immediate qualities of an environment, establishing links to a context of use that gave all phenomena deeper meaning; both place names and architectural terms disclose this process. Mythic geography was thus understood, down to its simplest elements. The world-image was both universal and local, and resulted in practice from the variation of common types, in accordance with place. This image is not reiterative of previous knowledge, but is in itself knowledge.[11] As being-in-the-world, we attain understanding through that which the Greeks called *techné,* or "knowing ability," which in our discussion corresponds to "building method." In this sense, all architectonic form has a "technical" basis. It follows, then, that building method gave rise to a tradition of building, which allows other customs to take place.

We have cited the gable as an example of the relation between building method and building tradition because it is characteristic of Nordic gestalt. It has its origins in wooden construction, and though post and ridge beam have parallels in southern architecture, the gable and the pitched or hipped roof are as characteristic of the North as the arch and the dome are of the South; this is confirmed by the Italian language's lack of a word for "gable." In its broadest sense, the gable is an anticlassical form that reaffirms the Nordic web.[12] This may occur, of course, in various ways, and with the aid of numerous methods of construction: the most important are half-timbering, log coursing, and stave construction. Further, we have seen that these building methods are conditioned not only by the dynamic gestalt of gable and spire but also by various roof forms, and cavelike interiors. In this way, both common Nordic and specific regional conceptions of the environment are expressed; they have in common that they are bound to the materiality of wood. Like nothing else, the tree represents, in root, stem, and crown, the unfinished Nordic world, where growth and tension replace the static eidos of the South.[13] The Nordic world is conserved and manifest when wood is employed as building material, even though there is always at issue

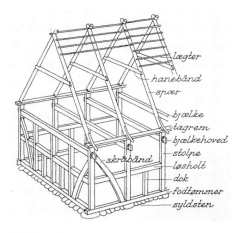

lægter
hanebånd
spær
bjælke
tagrem
bjælkehoved
stolpe
løsholt
dok
fodtømmer
syldsten
skråbånd

Half-timbering

a choice, among its particular qualities, with respect to the character of place. In general, wooden building is dynamic; its elements form a cooperative, elastic whole, reflecting the vital ramifications of wood. And correspondingly, the world is understood as an interplay of forces, rather than a collection of characters, and the interplay of forces results in moods. We can now examine how this understanding reaches expression in the four Nordic countries.

The origins of the Danish building tradition can be found in the building method known as half-timbering. As a system, it consists of frames, or two posts joined by a beam transverse through the building. This construction determines a bay width that is constant despite the total length of the building.[14] As such, it is an open form, which can satisfy diverse spatial requirements. In that it is a skeleton of horizontal and vertical frames, it can be more or less transparent, because windows and doors can be set in at will. It can be articulated in innumerable ways through the use of secondary links, varying junction points, and use of infill; as a result, its appearance shifts markedly from country to country and from region to region. Examples of half-timbering are the powerful, even brutal buildings in southwest Germany, the picturesque in Franconia and the Rhineland, and the orderly in Westfalen and Niedersachsen.[15] The simplest and clearest examples, however, are found in Denmark, where there is good reason to view them as significant attempts to accommodate place. In general, we can affirm that regional difference is highly characteristic, and that a trained eye can at once geographically place a half-timbered structure.

Danish half-timbering developed out of the earlier *bulhus* (log house) construction (*sleppvegg*), in which horizontal planks, or half-split logs, are "slipped" down in grooves between two bearing posts.[16] This plank structure was from earliest times combined with two sorts of interior bearing structures: the first is the aforementioned forked posts that support the ridge beam, known in Danish as *Sulehus* (post-house). The other is the *Højremshuset* (high-strip house), which employs two parallel rows of columns, one on each side of the ridge, that support a "strip" upon which the rafters rest. The high-strip house often has lower projections along the outer wall and can thus adapt to varying plans. Both the post-house and high-strip house have as a rule half-timbered outer walls, though half-timbering generally requires no interior support. These construction systems comprise roofs that appear as pitched and gable, half-hipped, and hipped.

There are significant regional variations; primarily, a distinction should be drawn between Zealandic and Jutlandic half-timbering. In Zealand, where access to stout timbers was limited, the structures are often slight and wide bayed, with few secondary links, and without continuously running foundation sills. Moreover, a difference in detailing exists from north to south: in south Zealand, transverse beams are tenoned through the

Zealandic half-timbering

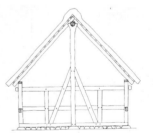

Danish roof construction

Zealandic half-timbering

"Gård," True, near Århus, Denmark

Jutlandic half-timbering

supports of the outer wall, whereas in the north, the two are lapped. Jutlandic half-timbering, conversely, is marked by an abundance of heavy timbers; not only are posts thicker, but the infill panels under windows are often subdivided by several secondary struts, and a stout foundation sill links the frames. In addition, this powerful skeleton is often emphasized through the use of color. In eastern Slesvig, a German influence can be seen: each post is furnished with diagonal bracing against the foot sill, and eaves rest on profiled brackets.

What, then, are the spatial and gestaltic consequences of the Danish building method? We have seen that half-timbering is principally an open system that can satisfy diverse spatial requirements through addition, and because the Danish farm house is typically one-storied, this is of essential importance. A well-known example is the farmhouse at Egen village on the island of Als, which stretches 238 feet.[17] This open system is constructionally well suited to the common *firlænge* as well. Openness entails, however, that the whole remains relatively undefined, and as a result, figurative unifying roofs were deemed necessary. The rhythmic order of walls and the large figurative roof form together a characteristic gestalt that is the mark of the Danish building tradition. In tandem with an intimacy of scale within an ordered whole, these qualities determine the Danish landscape, and in this way, the Danish house is simply and directly a world-image. This image is reinforced through detailing. There is a total absence of plasticity and drama: windows are neither high nor low but rest comfortably in the wall-plane; entry is not specifically stressed but occurs without disruption through the skeleton. These structures simultaneously create stillness and charm, which seems a continuation of the environmental qualities. Regional variants do not challenge these general qualities but nonetheless accommodate special local needs; thus hipped roofs are common along the coast and pitched roofs are found inland. Another example is offered by the high-strip house with projections, which protects the bearing structure against wind and weather in the harsh north Jutland climate. This type is also related to other earlier post-houses around the North Sea, suggesting that Denmark, too, is part of an Atlantic context.[18]

European urban building commonly has its roots in the rural settlement. This relationship is clearly demonstrated in Denmark's urban buildings that bear the impress of half-timbering's orderly rhythms, its surface treatment, and detailing. This basic tradition resonates even when in classical guise, or when rendered in masonry. As such, common Danish architecture illustrates the implications of a tradition of building and hints at solutions with respect to the problems entailed in translating from construction to form. This tacit relation is a result of the primary simplicity of the Danish tradition; here, one can sense a self-evidence, for historical development follows a clear sequence. Thus the Danish architectural historian Christian Elling speaks of "the strength of the artistic whole in Copen-

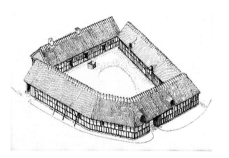

Danish "firlænge," True (now at the Lyngby Museum, Copenhagen)

Street in Copenhagen

Swedish log cabin from Dalarne

Urban Danish house

hagen," and continues, "the ideal street is ligated, and its space confined by facades of like height. The buildings' major coursing should run in unbroken lengths, uniting rows of windows. The single house should engage as a linear section of a longer building."[19]

Finally, it must be noted that the Danes have been successful in conserving their tradition of building into the present time. Jørn Utzon has been mentioned in this connection, and we can add that his housing complexes, such as the Kingo houses in Helsingør (1958–59), give convincing new interpretations of the Danish tradition. We might also add many other contemporary examples, but shall leave that until our final chapters. Let us simply state that Danish contemporary architecture demonstrates that the domestic and the modern admit conjunction.

This conjunction of domestic and modern has had a certain degree of success in Sweden, as well, whose building tradition is still integral with the character of the surroundings. Here, however, we will have to discover other origins; whereas Danish architecture has roots in half-timbering, it is log construction that has defined Swedish building and massivity replaces the structural skeleton.

Our investigation of what this implies for Swedish building tradition must be introduced by a brief look at log construction as a building method.[20] Its basic element is not the transverse frame but an embracive rectangle of stacked timbers. The Swedish word for this construction, *knuttimring,* reveals that this method acts like a "knot-ring" around space. There is reason to believe that log construction came to Scandinavia from the east: Russian has its word for this constructive unit, *srub,* and the Russian *izba* (house) consists of several such *sruby.* If we designate log construction as massive, it is because it functions as bearing wall: each element is equally important. This means that openings must be cut out, in contrast to half-

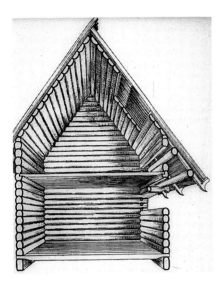

"Cave of wood," Härbre, Krakberg, Sweden

timbering, which is potentially open over all. Holes in bearing walls have a limited size because they tend to weaken the construction; moreover, timber ends that are exposed by cutting must be rebound to prevent slippage. Roof constructions in this context are principally of two kinds: *purlins* spanning gable to gable, or *rafters* that span from the sides to rest upon the ridge beam. When purlins form a continuation of the long wall up into the roof, a more closed effect results than with rafter construction. Purlin roofs are commonest in northeast Europe, and often the purlins are so tightly spaced that a cavernous space results, a method that is also in evidence in Sweden, giving Swedish log construction an eastern tinge. (Also eastern is the construction of roofs wholly of wood.) In contrast to Russian log construction that employs round timbers, adzing became common in Sweden, with the squared timbers forming a unified surface. Adzing prepared the way for the use of a somewhat regular standing panel cladding, the so-called locklistpanel (vertical clapboard). With this, gestalt quality is interpreted as a whole, geometric volume, which "forgets" its constructive origins. This gathered form was later emphasized through the use of the "broken gable"; and while it is possible that this roof form may result from the influence of the French mansard roof,[21] it is, irrespective of its origin, essentially suited to the Swedish kullar, and, as such, contributes to the development of a domestic tradition of building. Finally, the unified aspect of the Swedish house has been emphasized, since the seventeenth century, by the application of "barn red" as a unifying color.[22]

In the North, the introduction of log construction meant that larger single-unit houses, such as the post-house and the high-strip house, extant earlier in many areas, were subdivided into smaller units, limited by the length of available timber; as such, houses approach the *megaron* type. With the addition of an antechamber and removal of the entrance to the long wall, the plan develops into what Swedes call the *mora* type (known in Norway as the three-room plan). This type accommodates the addition of another room on the other side of the antechamber and thus becomes a *parstuga* (double house).[23] This is the origin of the *längor* (long house), found also in two-storied versions. In all cases, the outer wall is treated as a continuous surface, in accordance with the original interpretation of log construction; this is evidenced by the proportions of the wall surface and the sporadic openings. Instead of the Danish repetition of bays, a unified volume here appears, with applied accent.

Swedish folk architecture is not expressed in general structures but is instead defined by secondary but conspicuous motifs that advance figurally from the background of the wall. The roof does not appear as a unitive, figurative element, of the kind we saw in connection with half-timbering, but is engaged within the volume of the house proper. A rectangular Swedish tun is thus substantially different in character from the Danish. Here, the house is an independent unit, even though it may later be joined together

Swedish "double house"

Street in Linköping, Sweden

"Delsbogården" Hälsingländ (now at Skansen, Stockholm), Sweden

Square in Linköping, Sweden

with others; wholeness, then, is attained by the use of comprehensive wall treatment and coloration. "The color red is very dense in the Swedish landscape, here and there, linking together groups of houses. . . . The manor house is red, the outhouse is red, the laundry house is red, the slaughterhouse is red, the barns are red, and the cow shed is red."[24] In summary, we may say that the Swedish building tradition reinterprets northern European log construction as a more general, abstract conception of volume and surface. It is a field for motifs that express both regional and temporal differences. The basic gestalt quality remains surprisingly constant, considering the country's extent.

Sweden's urban environment is also affected by the rural settlement. We find the same elementary volumes, continuous surfaces, and sporadic openings that are glazed close to the outer edge. Applied motifs from monumental architecture—for example, the characteristic round corner tower—do not confound the general character; the result is a mood that is clearly distinct from the rigorous order of the Danish street. Whereas the Danish street is marked by ordered reiteration, Stockholm's Gamla Stan (Old Town) is distinguished by rich and varied detail. Contact with the countries around the Baltic Sea is unmistakable: one can see Baltic, Polish, even Bohemian features. As a result, Swedish building tradition is highly anticlassical, and the classical consists of reminders rather than comprehensive order. In general, this Swedish accentuation of volume and surface gives the gestalt an earthbound impression, though without chthonic weight.

We have remarked that Sweden, too, has had its share of success in unifying the domestic and the modern, as a result of both its unitary building tradition and of its capacity to assume new impulses through eclectic application. The country was unable, however, to assume modernism's more radical aims, such as Frank Lloyd Wright's destruction of the box. Modern Swedish architecture has remained for the most part bound to the simple closed volume and its empirical suppositions. Treatment of these issues, however, can be postponed to our last chapters.

Finland's folk architecture is closely related to that of the Swedish, as a result of both their common eastern origins and the direct influence that was brought to bear upon Finland under Swedish rule. These two factors brought about a division of characteristics that corresponds to the land's own division into coast and inland regions.[25] Inland, and eastward toward Russia, log construction holds its own and tends toward diffuse grouping of buildings. Coastally, however, and especially at the southern end of the Gulf of Bothnia, settlements display Swedish features: rectangular tun and double-chamber mora clad in clapboard, painted barn red. An authentically Finnish tradition of building must thus be sought inland, where we encounter characteristic gestalt in the form of primitive log construction. Whereas later Swedish building developed toward larger units, the Finnish retained the original

"Loft," Kurssi, Sydösterbotten, Finland

"Gård," Österbotten, Finland

Urban house, Porvoo (Borgå), Finland

Oulu, Finland

Yli-Laurosela, Ilmajoki, Österbotten, Finland

Finnish store houses

division into single houses with simple functions, placed in the landscape in an ostensibly irregular manner. The lack of distinct *place* in Finland's extensive forests impinges unquestionably upon this development; the closed grouping has no existing model in the natural environment. As a necessary complement, the house is conceived as a cave of wood, a place of refuge from open endlessness. In Karelia, the great Russian house appears, with living quarters and haylofts forming a high story over cow sheds and storage rooms.[26] Although this type advances into an originally Finnish region, nevertheless it cannot be said to represent a true Finnish building tradition.

An airy openness permeates Finland's urban settlements. Frequent conflagration necessitated broad streets, but though this requirement obtained throughout Scandinavia, nowhere has this need been so accommodated as in Finland. For despite a customary building height of one and a half stories, an extensive openness dominates. Under Russian rule in the nineteenth century, a detailing developed that outwardly distinguishes the buildings from Swedish folk architecture. This consists of the division of wall surfaces into horizontal bands: a solid plinth of standing panels below the fenestration, an extended fenestration band, and an attic frieze on top. In this manner, the coherence of volume dissolves, and this is further emphasized by exuberant Russian window surrounds and other details of carpentry. The tendency toward a dispersed and extensive horizontal gestalt also comes across clearly in the use of coloration: street facades were thus treated as applied screens, generally yellow, while end and back faces were red. The yellow front was, perhaps, an element of status, but nevertheless, the disintegrative whole that results is emphatically Finnish. Despite its simplicity, common Finnish architecture has a potential freedom in accordance with the unfinished land's possibilities. This freedom distinguishes the Finnish tradition of building from Denmark and Sweden's more established formal language and opens itself for a versatile relation to modernism.

In this century, Finnish architecture found its identity: its roots, first revealed by the *Kalevala,* were concealed beneath the influences of Swedish and Russian rule. But precisely because Finnish architecture is young, it has an especially strong relationship to its tradition of building. Tradition does not imply the reiteration of conventional forms, however, but reinterpretation of basic Finnish qualities. This occurred with convincing power, at the turn of the century, in the work of the architects Lars Sonck and Eliel Saarinen. Their work will be discussed more thoroughly later, but we can point out here some essential features. In the work of both architects, the Finnish sense of form is unmistakably present in their buildings' composed exterior gestalt and cavelike interiors. The Finnish log construction is an evident source of inspiration but is generally combined with masonry reminiscent of the Finnish Middle Ages.[27] Of special interest is the use of granite, the Finnish domestic stone, and though this may seem to have little to do with Nordic wooden architecture, we should remember that stone is omnipresent in Finland—not as cliff or mountain but as solid ground. From this emerges the land's web—such as Sonck's stonework: vital organic forms, seemingly concealed within granite, break forth and redefine this material in a Nordic manner. Thus, the tradition of building is not applied from without but emerges from within.

While folk architecture in Denmark, Sweden, and Finland has unambiguous roots, the tradition of building in Norway is more compound. Here as well, log construction is of primary importance, but, in addition, stave construction acts as an essential factor in the creation of form; it is thus a combination of these two systems that characterizes Norwegian folk architecture.[28] Its log construction is akin to the Swedish and Finnish and entered Norway from the east. The spatial unit is also the rectangle of embracive timbers, and roofing is of both rafter and purlin types. But the detailing is so distinct that it is of an entirely different order than that of Norway's eastern neighbors. In the east, timbers are subsumed within the coherent surface of the wall, whereas the Norwegian laft is based on individually plastic timbers. This system applies, for the most part, to main buildings such as cottages and lofts, while outbuildings are generally more primitively formed. A special characteristic is the so-called oval adzing, a labor intensive method whereby timbers are hewn to a vertical ovoid section, so that they appear to rise in space while remaining part of the embracive enclosure. An implicit tension is present in the undulatory line of stacked log ends, which extend progressively in an arc that forms the cantilever brackets for eaves or outer galleries. This dynamic reaches further expression in vertical doorposts that ligate the timbers loosed by the cut out opening. These posts appear in many different, but typical, variations; common to all is the expression of the meeting of rising and bearing forces. Here, the eastern "cave of wood" is redefined as space that envelops and rises. This can be seen in roofing: while the ridge-beam type is commonest toward the eastern border to Sweden, purlin and rafter types are found in middle and western Norway. In the Norwegian open hearth cottage, the smoke vent seems like a tear in the cloudy Nordic sky, remarkably open and closed at the same time.[29]

Stave construction is a skeletal system, distinct from log construction in that the bearing elements are vertical staves, or masts. They are chamfered over a ground sill and bear an upper "stave ledge," upon which the trusses rest. The interstices between staves in the outer wall are filled by standing planks, but the masts remain otherwise unbraced. Stave construction distinguishes itself from half-timbering in that it is based on straight-grained pine timbers, whereas half-timbering employs deciduous trees and must often rely on short, gnarled timbers. This difference is amply demonstrated by the great dimensions of the stave church, in its emphasis on verticality, and in its greater potential openness. Stave construction found its most complete expression in the stave church but was also employed in lofts

Kruke, Heidal, Norway

Kruke, Norway

Cottage, Gardsjord, Rauland i Telemark, Norway

and cottages, lending an interplay to the core of logs, and determining these structures' characteristic figure.

Norwegian building tradition is, in its origins, bound to this combination of stave and log construction; together, they provide rich possibilities for a varied architectonic expression, suited to diverse programs, given environments, and temporal concerns. Norwegian wooden architecture shows that it was capable of harnessing these possibilities. Programs have remained principally unchanged since medieval times, and it is of great interest to see precisely how the accommodation of temporal and local factors occurred. We have remarked that Norway's great differentiation of regions demanded varying tun types, and we can add that this variation is matched by a corresponding variation in built form.[30] The airy stave construction is common in Vestland; the cavelike loft appears in the eastern border regions. Between these two poles, we find various combinations from region to region, even from valley to valley. It is not possible here to examine these in detail, but we can mention that such major regions as Setesdal, Telemark, Numedal, Hallingdal, and Gudbrandsdal convincingly manifest the naturally given surroundings, consisting of variation of common basic themes, such as the three-room cottage and the loft. Variations also comprise interior treatments, which are typologically similar throughout. This combination of unity and multiplicity renders Norwegian folk architecture the unchallenged high point of European wooden architecture.

This is clearly demonstrated by the loft.[31] As a building type, it has remained unchanged throughout centuries, consisting principally of a timber wall core in two stories. The lower floor serves for the storage of food, while the upper space is used for the storage of clothes and as a sleeping loft in the summer. A cantilevered gallery, borne on brackets formed by the extension of log ends, extends from the timber core. In Telemark, this gallery runs around all four sides and emphasizes the building's corporal identity. In Numedal, it embraces only three sides and lends directionality. And in Gudbrandsdal, it covers only the entry face, revealing that here the tun takes precedence over the individual building. In Telemark and Numedal, the gallery was introduced simultaneously with foundation stumps. The gallery contrasts with the timber core and results in an assembly of dynamic ambiguity. Simultaneously light and heavy, closed and open, the loft reveals the nature of the land, where life takes place. As a "treasure chest," it preserves the soil's harvest and expresses humankind's creative power. As loft, it rises in space and tells of the fertile union of earth and sky. The horizontal timbers echo the expectant soil, while the gallery receives light from above. Articulation unifies the stave and loft systems, the springy curve of ovoid timber ends arc to support the gallery, a flange hovers in expression of growth and ephemerality, staves blur the distinction between above and below. Here, building tradition has truly become an art of building! Such is Jarand Rønjom's loft at Kleivi in Åmotsdal (1783).[32] In this building, each part

Open hearth cabin, from Åmli in Setesdal (now at
the Norwegian Folk Museum, Oslo)

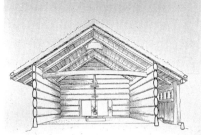

Section through an open hearth cabin

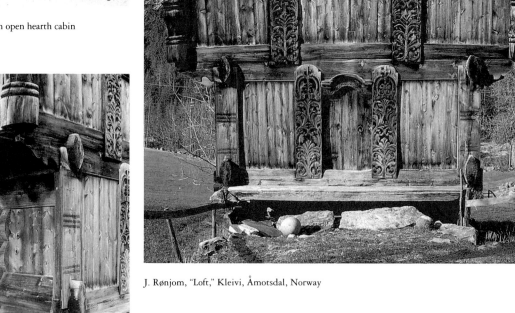

J. Rønjom, "Loft," Kleivi, Åmotsdal, Norway

J. Rønjom, "Loft," Kleivi, Åmotsdal, Norway

expresses its role in the whole, and the whole reifies an understanding of the Norwegian environment. But it is important to note that the loft is purely the result of building method. Thus in old Norwegian wooden architecture the translation to a more general language of form is only partially accomplished.

The building type in Trøndelag falls outside the descriptions we have sketched above; here, we find the rectangular tuns of the Swedish variety, which lends them a stronger identity. The urban architecture here takes up some of the issues raised in connection with Finland. In this way, Trondheim's streets have a sense of unified openness that realizes the region's rural settlement in urban form, while they echo Russo-Finnish wood detailing. This is not the place to account for the Norwegian "wooden city," but we can mention that the Norwegian condition is more complex than those of its neighbor lands, as a result of both regional differences and external influences.[33] A characteristic example of regional diversity is Bergen, where scale, character, and gestalt of the old settlement harmonize with the mobile topography of the local surroundings, and where Hanseatic influence is also felt. The general dynamism that otherwise marks the Norwegian building tradition emerges in the Østland's panel buildings, which with their robust impression resulting from split panels, broad gable boards, and strong detailing suggest how the methods of stave and loft construction can be realized as a valid language of form.

Norwegian building tradition has not been as amenable as the Danish or Swedish to unification with the modern. This is undoubtedly the result of its compound and ambiguous character, and of its incomplete liberation from original methods as well. Norway is the most "difficult" of the Nordic lands with respect to nature, and this is reflected in the lack of certainty among its modern architects. We return to this issue in later chapters, but mention that the country's tradition is now due serious consideration. The desire to create a modern Norwegian architecture can be seen in the establishment of the Wood Prize "for good architecture [which] call[s] forth those values that yet inhabit wood" in 1961, and the work of the numerous architects awarded the prize has offered a valuable contribution to the development of authentic typologies, although no clear direction has yet been staked out.[34]

Our treatment of Nordic building traditions has shown how the natural can become domestic with the aid of a suitable architecture; it has also shown that the domestic finds expression in characteristic spatial forms, buildings, and gestalts, and that these are the objects of our orientation, identification, and recognition. We have traced domestic building traditions from their origins in building method as a form of understanding, and pointed out that understanding occurred in different ways in the four Nordic lands, in accordance with their environmental character, while a common Nordic fea-

Stave and log construction, Langlim, Telemark, Norway

ture lies in the dependence on wood. Subsequently, we saw that methods of building developed into languages of form that conserved their validity despite the development of technical execution. It is this language of form that remains through the vicissitudes of temporal change, not as cumulative prototypes but as a more deeply founded attitude about space, form, and gestalt. Therefore, the word *appearance* should not be interpreted too literally but rather as that character that finds expression in manifold modes.[35] Building tradition thus connotes an open yet bounded manifold of interpretive possibilities. When these are employed in resonance with the demands of time, life may take place, and tradition may, in the best case, be realized as architecture. But it must be emphasized that the word *demands* is not primarily concerned with material needs but with the necessity for each period to establish a friendly relationship with the given place. Only in this way can the domestic become our own identity and allow us to say: "I am Norwegian," or "I am Danish."

Folk architecture expresses the immediately domestic; but the immediate has always had a universal basis, and this is maintained, as we shall see in the next chapter, by buildings other than those that serve everyday life.

"The wharf" in Bergen

Street in Trondheim

St. Karin, Visby on Gotland, Sweden

Most buildings in a cultural landscape serve the functions of everyday life. But those that do not are generally situated so that they are visible from a distance, evidently to act as a landmark and focus. The landscape assembles around them; they foster anticipation and draw us nearer. Such were the ancient temples, such are Islamic mosques, such are Europe's churches, and though these buildings serve differing world views, they have in common that they are *centers* where the unity of life and place reach essential expression. As such, they operate as *goals* and provide us with the experience of reaching something that explains the environment as well as our own existence.

The center is potential in nature itself; sometimes it is a rise or mountain dominating a landscape, sometimes a "space in space" where environmental factors seem concentrated; in other situations, it may be a place where we encounter the characters of the naturally given. From the earliest times, the central building has served to represent these relations. The Greek acropolis and agora represent the first two situations, whereas Delphi is an exceptional place where society, aided by architecture, addressed the given.[1] In all cases, praxis and meaning are integrated, for meaning is formed precisely when an environment is employed in a manner that manifests understanding, respect, and care, and the center is of primary importance for such an "understanding use." Europe's old cities demonstrate this: granted, bridges are placed where it is expedient to cross a river, but they also gather the surrounding land into meaningful place. But though the bridge may be the origin of a place, it is no goal; the goal must be a point where movement may fall to rest. This point can be established on one side of the river or both, so that a double center is formed. This is the case in Prague, where the old market lies on the east bank of the river and the castle on the west, while the famous Charles Bridge (1353) spans the two areas. Here again we can detect the types represented by acropolis and agora, but a third element is also present: the special "explanatory" building, for both market and castle have a church as a landmark.[2]

That is how it is everywhere in Europe: churches stand as an expression of human understanding. They assemble the land around themselves and give it tone. In this way, they represent the acknowledgment of a "here," and bring the inhabited landscape close to society. But do not all buildings achieve this? Yes—each in its own way; but whereas everyday buildings show us the earth as a "place to be," the explanatory building—temple, church, mosque—has a further aim: to represent the universal, that which is common to all places, and thus give a particular place its meaning as an "instance." In the three examples named, we see that the universal is anything but unambiguous; instead, it is based on *choice*. Denmark's stepped gable churches, Sweden's thickset towers, Finland's freestanding belfries, and Norway's spires confirm that with respect to the church, the matter is of *interpretation*.

4

The Universal

Stone church, Gotland, Sweden

What, then, do we mean by the term *universal?* If we recall the phrase "life takes place," the answer lies close at hand. The "universal" simply designates the basic structures of life and place. We have already recognized the structure of place as a cooperation of space, form, and gestalt; further, we have defined the structure of life as orientation, identification, and recollection and have shown that the two are inseparable; indeed, they constitute a whole that is called "being-in-the-world." But let us not forget that this, in practice, requires ever new choices and interpretations of the basic structures. These choices and interpretations are both temporally and locally dependent. Since the basic structures are our being-in-the-world, they are synonymous with human nature, and thus with the "fore-conception" mentioned earlier.[3] Fore-conception is that which allows for the possibility of seeing something as something; that which, in our discussion, allows for the comprehension of the structure of the surroundings. As human beings, we comprehend through orientation in space, identification with built form, and the recollection of gestalt. The result of this "understanding use" is a complex of goals, ways, and areas.[4] Martin A. Hansen provides us with an image of the "existential space" that this implies:

> One can ascend the tower of a country church and look out over the landscape from there. . . . Even today, one can see how the civilized landscape lies like a huge wheel, whose hub is the city. The axle is the church. Everywhere one sees paths and fences which move through the city like the spokes of a wheel. But 700 to 800 years ago, this wheel image was even clearer, and when a Romanesque farmer stood here like this, he could see life itself stream out over the farms, through rings of plots, and farther out over the meadows, divided by ridges and redivided in innumerable fields. Farther without lay half-open grazing land.[5]

As the center of existential space, of the landscape, the church acted as an axle around which all revolved, from whence life of place issued. It could play this role, empowered as it was by its explanatory quality. So says Mircea Eliade: "The ancient conception of the temple, as an imago mundi that reflects the essential in the universe, has been assumed by Europe's Christian churches . . . ," and further, "A universe is born at its center; it forms around a midpoint."[6] The world is formed, in other words, by the understanding that the center represents. This does not, of course, mean that it is the product of fantasy but, on the contrary, that it is an interpretation of the given, the durable. Every understanding is an understanding of "something"; and this something is, in our context, the given locality where life takes place and, in particular, the central place where the whole seems to be gathered: in earlier times such locations were called "holy places."

What, then, is the understanding of the unity of life and place represented by the church? Spatially, the Early Christian basilica maintains the "path of life," interpreted as "the path of salvation," from the profane world without toward the altar within. As such, it is a primarily longitudinal structure, with entrance and goal. But as a goal, the altar is also center, and this implicit centricity was soon emphasized by the use of transepts, and by raising a baldachin over the altar. Though the basilica is primarily linear in structure, centralization thereby came to play an essential role.[7] Movement forward in this space occurs "on earth under heaven," and this is expressed in a characteristic built form that manifests the meaningful relation between above and below. Anthropomorphic (classical) columns line the nave, screening the laminar aisle space behind, while the high wall above, through which light enters, appears as a dematerialized surface covered with mosaics. Here, classical inheritance is both employed and contradicted, in the service of representing a Christian world view. Additionally, "heavenly light," which emanates from above, is brought close to mortals through large apsidal windows.[8] The gestalt of the Early Christian church may be characterized as an introspective casing around space and form; but there were latent features that would be fundamental to further development: the west front as a symbolic threshold between the profane and sacred domains; the image of the long enveloping building that that stands like a ridge, gathering the landscape and city around itself; the nave crossed by transept, awaiting the emphasis of a tower; and the apse, embracing the goal, suggesting the possibility that its "message" radiate into the surroundings.

These are the basic features of how the church building offers a universal interpretation of our being-in-the-world. The history of sacred architecture is the history of the accommodation of the universal to the temporal and topical. And while it is not our task here to account for this process, let us mention that this accommodation occurs through varying syntheses of longitudinal and central spaces; by variation in the formal themes of the interior; through the formation of a meaningful outer gestalt, such as the tower and the cupola. This development has so far been presented for the most part within temporal terms, that is, as a progression of stylistic periods, while topical variation has been disregarded.[9] It is important for our architectural understanding, however, to investigate in what way the universal has set root under differing "expanses of sky."

As we saw earlier, expanses of sky within the North are numerous. We encounter therefore many differing manifestations of the universal; each demonstrates how the universal must take place in order to become real. A journey through the North corroborates that churches are as locally defined as folk-architecture, though the universal still becomes manifest; as a result, the study of sacred architecture provides essential insight into the Nordic as well as shedding light on the universal. Differences emerge already in the situation of buildings. As a function of geography, landscape elements vary,

Kundby, northwest Zealand, Denmark

Elmelunde, Møn, Denmark

Elmelunde, Møn, Denmark

and thence the "holy places" where the church belongs. The problem of localization, however, has not been examined in depth, and we must here content ourselves with some suppositions.

Denmark's conditions are the simplest; as we have seen, the churches there lie on the low hills that are characteristic of the country and that afford broad view. Our quotation from Martin A. Hansen is appropriate with respect to both cultural landscapes in general and the Danish condition in particular. Characteristic examples are Elmelunde on Møn and Kundby in North Zealand; the latter is known in those parts as "the visible church." In general, we can say that Danish place, which has a relatively weak definition with respect to nature, requires a great degree of centricity in order to complement what is missing. The church accomplishes this task through meaningful gestalt; as such, it is not only a building but also an exterior space bounded by conspicuous walls that limit the microcosm of the churchyard against the surroundings. But this border does not divide two worlds; instead the precise churchyard hedges serve as a symbolic visualization of the landscape's "concealed" structure. Central in this space, the church itself stands like an embodiment of the hill's rise; without drama, its balanced geometry receives light and shows us that in this land, heaven and earth coexist in harmony.

Svealand's landscape elements are not especially clear in definition, as a result of the labyrinthine mixture of kullar and pasture. Here, space must also be bounded, and place must be emphasized through a gestalt that can dominate the kullar. The first demand is impressed upon all building forms in this landscape: this is evident in the frequency of the suffix -tuna (tun), which might be called a courtyard farm or extended farm, in Swedish place names. Thus, the farm complex is at the origin of the Swedish place.[10] And here, too, the churchyard reflects this origin. It is not, as in Denmark, divided by low hedges, but instead has the quality of a continuous surface upon which the headstones stand. In order to establish the necessary presence of place, church buildings are emphasized with freestanding belfries or massive towers crowned with conspicuous finials. Here, the relationship of earth to sky is less resolved; the earth is seen as mass rather than as geometric order, and the sky remains something distant toward which humankind must aspire. Among Sweden's old church sites, Old Uppsala holds a special position where a slight rise in the expansive Uppland plains has been a holy place from earliest times. Its pagan temple was described by Adam of Bremen around 1070, and a half a century later it became the seat of a Christian bishopric. A large stone church was built, replacing the earlier wooden one.[11] Even today, Old Uppsala appears as a center; it informs us of the meaning of the central place in the cultural landscape.

In Finland, it is natural that centers be fixed in relation to the "thousand lakes" that form a network of communication throughout the extensive forests. In many places the church boats used as a means of transport are still extant; their size speaks of the former importance of the waterways, indeed, as a factor in the creation of place. Finland's churchyards are also bounded by walls, formed of massive blocks of stone that seem an echo of the stony earth. Already, this spatial boundary reveals the genius of place. Within the walls, the ground is like Sweden's continuous surfaces. Thereupon stand the belfry and church, as a rule independently, expressive of Finland's extensive spreading, and manifesting the double need for landmark and "cave." Wooden churches are particularly representative in this respect, such as the famous example in Petäjavesi.[12] Here again, we see that the naturally given is the point of origin for an "explanation" that has as its object to allow place to emerge as part of a universal context.

Stora Tuna, Dalarne, Sweden

In contrast with the other Nordic lands, Norway offers a multiplicity of naturally given places: valley, fjord, island. All of these possess natural centers, which may be noted in such place name suffixes as *stad* (place), *nes* (point), *vik* (cove), and *sund* (sound). Both the cove and the point are natural church sites in a landscape of fjords and inland lakes that also look like and are called "fjords." In valleys, however, it is necessary to determine a mid-point around which movement can fall to rest. Church buildings require a more dramatic form in order that they might stand out as centers in the harsh Norwegian landscape. This is amply demonstrated by the stave church and by the spires that came into use after the Reformation.[13] As a result of Norway's distinct structure of place, it is important to investigate its "holy" centers, both as a way of achieving a deeper understanding of place and in order to see what the Christian world view assumed from its pagan predecessors.[14]

Our remarks concerning the situation of churches in the North bear witness to the fact that the universal does not disclose itself directly but must be interpreted in relation to the here and now. Let us then investigate Norway's version of the church building more closely, so that we can better grasp what indeed the universal means.

No other building expresses the Nordic world to the degree that the stave church does; in this form, we discover precisely the anticlassic character the Norwegian landscape requires. Again, Martin A. Hansen gives us an unsurpassed description:

> One does not quickly comprehend the idea in such a building. Myriad roofs and gables compel the glance wildly upwards, till it springs from the spire to the heavens, piercing javelin-like. The church is a living, fantastic creature—wild, darkly glowing black, umber, ochre, gold; here and there, scaly like a monster, the shingles. It is foreign, demonically agitating, diabolically confounding. In the first instant, one asks oneself if this is at all architecture; in the next, the strange structure stands totally still, not heavily resting, but hovering as if weightlessly. The eye has yet to

Petäjavesi, Finland

decipher its lines, let alone understand its construction. Nothing is clear, but one understands when the eye has captured its dramatic theme; everywhere elements stretch and dissolve and radiate from the building; or rather, it is both tensive and liberative in relation to the great landscape around. . . . On the high broad door surrounds of very small doors, graven ornament flows in powerful motion. Also within, carvings and painted decoration sprout forth like a living stream on obscure surfaces. . . . There comes but little sunlight into the stave church. Some still have original windows, small round peepholes high up under the roof of the nave. The weak light is split by roofwork and sinks like a dim atmosphere into the room.[15]

This indeed says it all: living and fantastic, wild and tensive; lines and forms rising toward the sky, met there by dim light. The great landscape acts as both participant and spectator. The classically schooled Dane asks himself "if this is at all architecture." But his description is an implicit yes, for as a Nordic man, Martin A. Hansen feels a deep affinity with what he sees here, different though it is from that to which he is accustomed in his homeland.

But is it so certain that the stave church is Norwegian? Is it not established that it is a remnant of an extinct wooden architecture found not only throughout Scandinavia, but in Germany and England as well, indeed even in northern France? It is true enough that wooden churches were built in many places, and that nearly all disappeared with the advent of stone construction. In this respect, we are fortunate that sacred wooden medieval architecture survived in Norway; moreover, the Norwegian stave church was able to develop further, and in so doing achieved a greater degree of perfection. But there are flaws in this reasoning: first, the structure of churches in other countries was not stave construction; and second, the Norwegian church was, so to speak, perfect from its inception.[16] As such, it has been impossible to demonstrate a development in Norwegian stave construction, except that the introduction of foundation-frame sills around 1100 represented an unquestionably important technical advance. But it is not the ground frame that makes a building a stave church, just as stump and sill do not make the Norwegian loft what it is.

Urnes, Norway

Borgund Stave Church, Norway

Gol Stave Church (now at the Norwegian Folk
Museum, Oslo)

What, then, is the true distinguishing feature of the stave church? To find it, we need to look to the roof rather than at the ground—and that is indeed natural in a church. Under the roof, then, we find a sort of "lace collar" of stiffening spandrels, which in concert with the frame of staves, forms a raised baldachin.[17] The effect achieved by the varying number of staves that are carried from this collar downward to the ground is sometimes more, sometimes less centralized, though all are in principle centralized spaces. The baldachin structure is the stave church's basic gestalt, and its interior is accordingly quite different from that of the Early Christian nave. It is thus erroneous to state that "the Norwegian columnar stave church is the stone basilica retold in wood, without the least trace of any older domestic element."[18] In order to retell, one requires a language, and it is evident that the stave church had just such a language at its disposal—namely, a highly developed building method. This can only be a domestic element, not introduced with the church, but stemming from older local building, most likely from the much-discussed pagan temple.[19] Should a temple be transformed into a church, one need only add a chancel, and thereby gain the oblong emphasis required for Christian services. The main space, however, retains its centricity, and an unclear transition to the chancel results; this relation corroborates that we are not in the presence of a retelling. The importance of the stave church is not weakened because it stems from the temple; rather, it is this continuation that reveals its domestic roots and makes the new universality comprehensible. Both the temple and the church have a task to "explain" the environment, and must therefore employ related means. There is even a question whether the stave church has adequately completed this transformation into a Christian church. Roar Hauglid's book on the stave church, which defends the retelling theory, is introduced, strangely enough, with a citation from Holger Drachmann, which states that the Borgund church is "like a smokehouse dedicated to a mystic cult, wherein the darkness of the sagas overwhelms Catholicism's dimly burning votives."[20]

Thirty stave churches are more or less well preserved in Norway, of approximately one thousand that were built in the Middle Ages. Of these, Borgund (c. 1150) is the most complete and corresponds well to Martin A. Hansen's description. Borgund has twelve freestanding staves (in the "collar" there are fourteen), whereas other churches have four, eight, sixteen, even twenty if the outer walls are not loadbearing.[21] The typology may seem indefinite, but the recognition that they are all variations on the baldachin theme renders the whole meaningful and comprehensible. This principle can be seen clearly in the Valdres churches Hurum and Lomen, in which upper collars of fourteen staves are supported by only four staves, one in each corner; here, the architectonic origin is evident, as building method, as space, as gestalt. But to understand the fantastic appearance of the stave church, we must see it as expressive of the secretive and dramatic Norwegian envi-

Lomen Stave Church, Norway

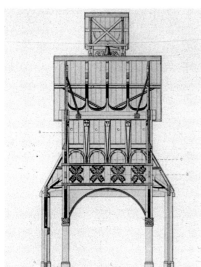

ronment; in concert with cottage and loft, it explains a whole. But whereas the cottage's log embrace and the loft's ambiguous rising illuminate the everyday, the stave church's vertical and open form expresses the ceremonial. And it is in the ceremonial that the universal takes place.

Despite its original and artistic qualities, the stave church found itself overshadowed. The primary manifestation of the universal in the Middle Ages was stone building, ushered in by Christianity. Scandinavia's master builders had little in the way of tradition at their disposal with respect to stone construction, and as a result, the first structures were rather primitively executed, such as Tveje-Merløse in north Zeeland, from 1090. It was only after the establishment of the first archbishopric in Lund, in 1104, that stone construction reached a European level; but here, the master builder was a Lombard![22] The development of Nordic sacred stone architecture, then, took place in the twelfth century, that is, in the Romanesque period. This occurred in parallel in Denmark, Sweden, and Norway. In Finland, which was still but an outpost, the first stone churches stem from around 1250.[23] If we include the following Gothic period, it is estimated that some three hundred stone churches were built in Norway; the figures for Sweden and Denmark are notably larger: around two thousand for each. Thus medieval church building was extensive, and for our discussion it is possible to treat only some major features and investigate if, here too, the Nordic finds expression.

Its name informs us that the Romanesque springs from Roman prototypes, that is, the Early Christian basilica, as it developed in Rome from about 320 onward. But from the beginning, Romanesque architecture showed a tendency to break with its late antique heritage. This break consists of the desire to provide an architectonic interpretation of the Roman basilica's dematerialized nave wall and its accompanying colonnade below. This entails that built form increasingly approaches the skeleton, a tendency that is a natural progression of the original intentions involved in the formation of the space of the church. Superficially considered, it might seem as though this occurred in a similar manner throughout Europe, for the Romanesque is often presented as an international style that is expressive of the unity of the Roman Catholic church. But we can also recognize characteristic variations that are in accordance with local *genius*. The Italian Romanesque, thus, is generally an outer "garment" that girds a traditional structural body (such as in Pisa), whereas the French sought to reinterpret the substance of the building itself, with significant consequences for both spatial organization and outer gestalt.[24] This occurred, however, without losing sight of the original; for it was precisely in the Early Christian basilica that the universal found its Christian interpretation; in the Romanesque church, the "path" motif as well as the distinction of below and above are retained. It is not surprising, then, that the development of the Romanesque found its epicenter in France, which is the only country that borders on both the Mediterranean and the North Sea (or at least its "gate.") Here, a classical

Kviteseid, Old Church, Norway

Tveje Merløse, Denmark

anthropomorphism is successfully joined with the Nordic skeletal structure, resulting in an architecture that gives the Christian-universal a new presence. This development culminated in the built form of the Gothic that appears as a web of lines of force.

Walter Horn has provided us with the key to this process: he points out that the medieval bay system could only develop at the rate that it did because of a preexistent building tradition.[25] This consisted of large-span wooden structures that could be repeated in length at will. We have already seen this type of construction in the previous chapter, that is, in the high-strip house, and many medieval halls based on this system are in existence today. Horn has measured and described a series of such buildings in northern France and England whose dimensions approach those of cathedrals.[26] He has also found that similar constructions are present in Holland, Flanders, and northern Germany and adds that at one time there must have stood thousands. The conclusion is that the medieval cathedral represents a synthesis of the monolithic Early Christian basilica and the transalpine wooden skeletal hall structure. Here again, we see that a domestic building method makes possible the roots of the universal, at the same time as building method becomes a formal language. It is, to be sure, in this regard that it has been remarked that the Gothic cathedral was raised "despite stone."[27]

How, then, did this development occur in the North? Nordic stone churches were at first very simple. In Denmark and Sweden, as well as in Norway, they consisted merely of a rectangular nave and a smaller square chancel; some had an apse, some did not. What is the reason for this formal poverty? The answer is simple: the lack of a stone building tradition made it difficult to develop an articulate formal language, and wooden architecture was of little help. As a result, foreign craftsmen were called in to build the cathedrals at Lund and Trondheim. In the first case, these workmen apparently came from the Rhineland (which in turn had its technical knowledge from Lombardy), and in the second, from England. Danish stone structures were thus from the outset German oriented, while the Norwegian counterparts found Anglo-Norman inspiration. The cathedral at Lund is generally considered the most significant Romanesque building in the North, with its magnificent Rhinish-Lombard apse (c. 1150) and ordered monumental interior.[28] The Romanesque transept at Trondheim (before 1150) is of an equal caliber; here, however, there is not the same logical system but instead a simpler, English superposition of well-detailed arched openings in a thick-walled envelope. Among the details, of particular note is the zigzag border known as *chevron,* developed around 1100.[29] The chevron is the Nordic form par excellence, in that it contradicts the classical arch, which associates the Romanesque with the Roman. Whereas in the South the arch seems to dissolve optically through the alternate use of light and dark stones, the chevron assails constructive substance itself. In Sweden, cathedral building began

Cathedral, Lund, Sweden

Nidaros Cathedral, Norway

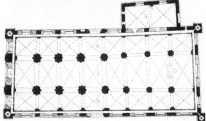

Cathedral, Västerås (original appearance), Sweden

with the establishment of bishoprics in Skara, Linköping, Eskilstuna, Strängnäs, Sigtuna, and Västerås in 1120. Soon thereafter, a Swedish pluralism formed. Influences are felt from Lund, from northern Germany, and from Anglo-Norman regions. In the following centuries, this multiplicity strengthened, while Denmark sought a less ambiguous, domestic, ecclesiastic architecture.

As time passed, forms borrowed from the cathedrals began to show up in simple country churches. This did not, however, occur by means of random duplication but as an attempt at articulation; at the same time, local features began to congeal. The common point of origin, the rectangular nave and square chancel, is a Nordic form with interesting possibilities for development, in that it anticipates the repetitive spatial structure of later stone churches. At Strängnäs and Västerås, the result was a uniform grid plan of undetermined extent, within an enclosing envelope. Similar plans mark Uppland's smaller churches; later this structure found its way into Finland. In Denmark, conversely, attention focused upon providing the church with an ordered exterior rhythm, an aim that should be considered in connection with the Danish building tradition in general. Here, brick came into use as a building material after 1160 and eased the development of an "adaptive" formal language.[30] At first it was used in connection with finer profiles in window and door surrounds, but it was soon employed as a basic building material for large buildings. In Sweden, and later Finland, the introduction of brick opened the way for influences from the northern German Backsteingotik (brick Gothic), and thereby for the development of a particular Baltic character. In Norway, some isolated echoes of Trondheim cathedral arose, but the main interest remained in wooden architecture; stone churches thus remained linked to their Anglo-Norman models.[31] With these general remarks in place, let us now look more closely at the individual contributions of the Nordic countries to the development of sacred stone architecture.

From the outset, Danish parish churches were marked by the concern for precise form.[32] In Jutland, this is manifest in ordered ashlar-cladding exteriors and plastered interiors. In Zealand, conversely, churches were built of the loose granite blocks conveyed here during the ice age, which were then plastered both within and without. Later, blind arcades, pilasters, and half-columns emerged, making possible a tighter, rhythmic articulation. Examples are Nørre Jernløse in northern Zealand, Hee near Ringkøbing, and Roager near Ribe, all from the twelfth century. The introduction of brick allowed the demand for ordered and rhythmic articulation to be met, and the church began to assume its characteristic Danish note. It was thus possible to give the simple Romanesque form a more distinct rhythm, particularly through the addition of stepped gables (*Kamtakker,* or "comb roofs") to towers and end walls. This configuration is also present in other countries, but in Denmark its significance appears as a reification of the latent repetitive structure of Denmark's tradition of building, as preconditioned by the

Maribo, Lolland, Denmark

Maribo, Lolland, Denmark

Bell towers at Mörkö, Sweden

Ytre Järna Church, Sweden

Härkeberga Church, Uppland, Sweden, exterior

Härkeberga Church, Uppland, Sweden, interior

Danish landscape. When Gothic ribbed vaults appeared within, the interior gestalt found its final form: as a friendly space under "trees," peopled with paintings of the Christian explanation of the meaning of life. Brick was also used for the large monastic churches in Sorø and Ringsted, begun in the 1160s, and the brick Roskilde cathedral followed some ten years after. Finally, Danish medieval architecture found a last grand interpretation in the Birgittine church in Maribo on Lolland (1416–70). Within the enclosing "heavenly ladder" of the stepped gables, we find a space stirring in luminous softness: over a continuous geometric floor rise massive octagonal pillars. They seem to lift earthly substance up through the vaulting, where the celestial is present in pure clarity.

In Sweden, conditions were more complex than in Denmark. Here, numerous influences converged, and the very extensity of the land required several distinct centers. Already in the Romanesque period, buildings were furnished with towers, generally on the west front, but also sometimes adjacent to the apse in the east. Moreover, freestanding belfries were common, and in order to withstand the vibrations caused by the church bells, they were constructed in forms that often seem complex and bizarre.[33] Hence the belfry stands in sharp contrast to the simple and resolved body of the church, and we can discern, in this contrast, the origin of the characteristic Swedish tower: a stout massive body crowned by a more freely formed bell receptacle. The freestanding belfry is, so to speak, raised up upon a mass of wall. In Uppland and Norrland, though, the freestanding tower is retained. This, too, is generally the case in Finland, and represents evidently a response to the forest environment. In both cases, the tower is of greater significance than in Denmark, where it is more or less absorbed into the stepped gables. A truly splendid formal development occurred on Gotland, though with obvious reference to German models. All in all, tower building culminated in the fifteenth century, when many Swedish cathedrals were provided with new dominant west towers in brick. If a church has a freestanding tower, its outer gestalt is defined to a great degree by the configuration of the west front; as a result, steep gables came into use. With the introduction of brick, the gable was generally appointed with rich patterns of blind windows, scissored arches, and chevron borders, as at the great brick church in Vendel in Uppland (1310). These are the characteristic motifs that we have designated *Baltic,* and while the term *Hanseatic* applies as well, it must be emphasized that the blind window motif in Sweden, Finland, and the Baltic regions never attained the same picturesque sense that is evident in northern Germany.

Swedish medieval churches, tended, as we have already seen, toward the aula type, wherein spaces of equal height are added in both length and breadth. The "antibasilican" interior that is thus formed has as its undoubted source of inspiration the Nordic "forest space."[34] There is the obvious influence, too, of Westfalen's hall churches, but the formal development of the vaults and their fresco decoration creates another character. These are akin to the Danish vaults mentioned before, but in Sweden there is an additional sense of indefinite extension. The cathedrals at Västerås, Strängnäs, Linköping, and the Great Church in Stockholm are such hall spaces, and the later-added chancel at Strängnäs offers a fascinating example of an interior where the decoration of the vaults effects a paradisical explanation of the Mälar valley environment. The cathedral at Uppsala conversely, falls outside of the Swedish development, representing as it does a conscious reaction to German influence. Begun in 1271 according to plans ordered from France, its ostensibly French appearance was stripped of much of its architectonic value by a heavy-handed restoration in the nineteenth century.[35]

Finland's medieval churches are not numerous, but they are of high quality. Inspired by Uppland architecture, their strong effect results from blind-windowed gables, unified building envelopes, and freestanding bell towers. Here, too, the plan is the result of an addition of equal spaces within an enclosing rectangle, whereby space seems both endless and cavernously closed. In this respect, the Finnish churches demonstrate how artworks can conjoin logical contradictions. Some of them are built in natural stone with brick gables (Parvoo (Borgå) 1415); others are completely of brick. Of the latter type, Hattula (first-half fourteenth century), with its triple nave and especially fine frescoes, is a worthy representative of the Finnish interpretation of the universal. Of interest is the local peculiarity of a weak division of upper and lower zones, in that the vaults continue unbroken down into the pillars that support them. Among Finnish medieval churches, the cathedral at Turku (Åbo) holds a special position:[36] Turku became an episcopal seat in 1259, and the church was begun soon after as a hall church with a distinctly Baltic character. A hefty west tower was, to all appearances, integral with the first plan, but it was heightened in the fifteenth century, and after the fire of 1827 it received its present closure by C. L. Engel. The interior was rebuilt in 1460; here, too, pillars and walls run contiguously, resulting in massive closure below and open furcation in the vault zone.

While regional features developed in Denmark, Sweden, and Finland, Norway's stone churches remained simpler, in a more original state. We have suggested that this was the result of the dominant interest in stave construction, an assumption confirmed by the great number of stave churches. Nonetheless, it is within Norway's borders that Nordic stone church building's most important and valuable example exists: the cathedral at Trondheim, known as the Nidaros Cathedral. It was begun around 1070 in the Romanesque style. After Trondheim became an archbishopric in 1153, the church gained significance, but it was only after 1180 that the original octagon was raised in connection with an expanded plan for the entire structure. The octagon was added to the nave as a martyrium for Saint Olav, Norway's martyr king. Olav worship was already widespread in Scandinavia, and churches in honor of Olav were built in many places, even as far away as Novgorod. Around 1230, the nave was completed, and in 1248

Cathedral, Strängnäs, Sweden

Hattula Church, Tavastland, Finland

work began on the west front. It is supposed that the church's main parts stood complete at the beginning of the fourteenth century.[37] The plan is of the English type, apart from the centralized eastern element, which is undoubtedly inspired by the Holy Sepulcher in Jerusalem.[38] The system of construction is related to other contemporary English cathedrals, in which a dense masonry core is optically dissolved by a "curtain" of applied column shafts and ribs (Lincoln, Salisbury); this intention is particularly evident in the west front's screen. The Nidaros Cathedral takes up these themes and develops them to their ultimate consequences. As such, the entire building is characterized by line rather than mass and surface. This is, of course,

Hattula Church, Tavastland, Finland

Cathedral, Turku (Åbo), Finland

Gothic, but few structures express the wooden origins of Gothic so clearly.[39] It is tempting to say that this is precisely why it possesses a distinct domestic character. This character also appears in innumerable fantastic details, reminiscent of the Danish poet Holger Drachmann's words on the Borgund stave church. Nidaros Cathedral has no parallel in the Nordic countries; it is, in essence, Nordic, but in a secretive manner that it is tempting to denominate Norwegian. Because of its architectonic quality, the cathedral functioned as a center for Trøndelag, and thereby for all of Norway, until the fire of 1328 destroyed much of it. For centuries it stood in a depleted state until restoration began in 1869. Meanwhile, in 1350, the Black Death arrested Norway's blossoming medieval culture.

Our treatment of Romanesque and Gothic sacred architecture in the Nordic countries shows how the church functioned as a center for the cultural landscape, and in order that it could be locally effective, it needed to accommodate a universal message to the local situation. This occurred when the building concentrated the qualities of the environs into a character that conserved and visualized them. In this way, the landscape was understood, and brought close to mankind. The character did not express a definite everyday action but instead represented a whole. For wholeness is another word for the universal. Here, it means particular manifestation of the universal earth-heaven relation that applies to all places. Martin A. Hansen's wheel image emphasizes the significance of the center, and the manifold character of the churches informs us that each landscape requires its own axle. In Denmark, the church seems a condensation of the ordered cultural landscape, and thus

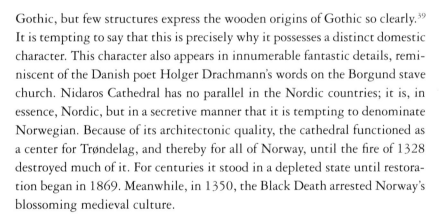

Cathedral, Turku (Åbo), Finland

represents its essence. In Sweden, it stands above all as a landmark, complementing that which the inscrutable environment lacks. In Finland, the cave is more important than the landmark, as a counterweight to the land's endless, yet hidden, extension. And in Norway, the focal building needs to be strong enough to confront the dramatic nature of the country. These indications grasp, however, only one side of a relation that is far more complex, but they do inform us that the universal is never directly manifest, but must *take place*.

Society requires focal buildings, since they are a life-giving source that emanates out into the surroundings. In anticipation, we carry them with us when we approach a goal, in the hope that their explanatory gestalt will render the experience a whole. In order to satisfy our anticipation, the space of building must respond to this orientation, its built form must express how we are on earth under heaven; and its gestalt must translate wholeness into a durable image. Throughout the centuries, the church managed to accomplish this through the unification of the universal with time and place.

Cathedral, Trondheim, Norway

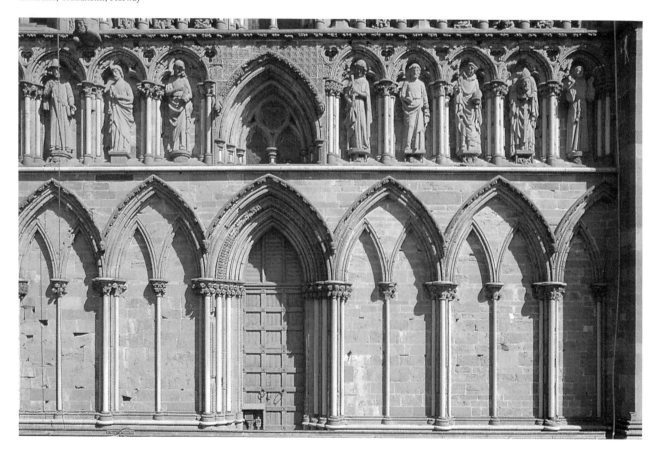

Cathedral, Trondheim, Norway

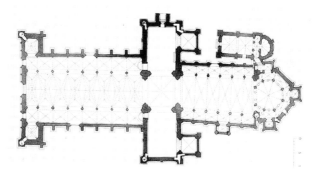

Tidö Castle, Sweden

Throughout Europe, classical architecture has impressed its forms upon the surroundings. Greek columns and temple pediments appear in both country and city; they are common enough that they often seem a part of the natural domestic building tradition. This has been the case not only in the past but in our own time as well, for as late as the 1920s, most buildings were designed in the classical style.[1] Scandinavia is no exception. Here, too, the classical is ubiquitous; the most important buildings of the capital cities are generally classical in guise, as in Copenhagen, Stockholm, and Oslo. Even Finland, which lies far from the Continent, offers one of Europe's most beautiful urban classical works: Helsinki's Senate Square (Senaatintori). But does this not contradict our hypothesis that Nordic architecture is otherwise—that here, the classical is foreign? Or is it perhaps that the classical is also something universal, and thus universally applicable?

Before arguing these questions, it should be noted that the classical style has not always been employed in the North. It first became common in the sixteenth century, in a rather domesticated guise, and it is important to note that this occurred at a time when the relatively cohesive medieval culture began to dissolve, primarily as a result of the loss of its monopoly status by the Roman Catholic church. As we know, Luther made public his Theses in 1517, and already by the 1520s the Reformation was in full swing in Sweden and followed soon after in Denmark and Norway, that is, in 1536–37. This entailed not only a religious upheaval but an enhancement of the significance of the power of the king as well. Rulers looked, from the first, to classical architecture as a means to manifest their position, a fact that has been understood as an attempt at a "cultural alibi."[2] Centralization of power, moreover, occurred concurrently with a concentration of the population, and the introduction of classicism was generally effected in connection with planned urbanization.[3] Houses, too, were often ornamented with classical motifs, again as an expression of status. There is undoubtedly some truth in these explanations, but a satisfactory understanding lies deeper. The forms of architecture, even in misuse, are always "world images"; further, we have seen that the classical has its origins in a definite understanding of the world. Let us therefore look more closely at this understanding before we take up the issue of the foreign in the North.

We have seen that the classical is a manifestation of the comprehensive and unitary sun-space of the South, wherein all things appear as corporal presence, and that the thing's individuality is defined by its eidos or aspect. An aspect is, above all, a function of contour or outline, and a world of distinct elements consists moreover in definite classes that share a particular eidos. Among these, the human body is especially significant, and the world image of Greek architecture consisted primarily in the representation of human character: its basic element is the anthropomorphic column, which in its various guises—Doric, Ionic, Corinthian—represented masculine and feminine traits. But the column does not *depict* the human body, despite its

Rosenborg Palace, Copenhagen

occasional replacement with human figures; it instead translates basic human qualities into built form. The contour of this form interprets the relation to the earth as the base, the relation to the heavens as the capital, and can thus express essential differences of character within the limits of the body's manner of presence.[4] The contour is, moreover, defined in proportion to the gestalt it completes, and therefore the classical is always bound within certain ideal numerical relations. Finally, an order of this sort entails repetition of like essences and thereby clear, elemental, and geometric spatial organization; its common criterion is the understanding that all individual things are reflections or shadows of ideal archetypes.[5] The idea informs the singular case whose aim is to approach as nearly as possible the basic type. In this event, the individual becomes "divine," that is, representative of an eternal and complete order.

Our understanding of the thought behind Greek architecture is due to the architect Vitruvius, a contemporary of Augustus Caesar. As a result, the classical tradition is generally referred to as "Vitruvian," and though subject to many variations through time, its basic propositions have retained their validity.[6] When classical forms regained dignity and favor once again after the Middle Ages, it was thus appropriate to speak of a Renaissance. The following baroque style was also essentially classical—especially as seen in the work of the period's leading artistic figure, Gian Lorenzo Bernini. The Vitruvian tradition applies not only to form as such but also to the meaning

Rosenborg Palace, Copenhagen

of forms. As a result, contents based initially on the anthropomorphism of the Greek gods were translated into Christian terms; thus, churches dedicated to male saints took on the Doric style, whereas those dedicated to the Virgin Mary assumed the Ionic. City gates and defense fortifications were Doric, representative monumental buildings Corinthian. Hence the classical truly functioned as a language based on a vocabulary of meaningful forms.[7] An exposition of this system, however, is not the task at hand; here we are concerned with the reasons that the classical language came to the North and an investigation of how its meeting with the Nordic influenced its means of expression.

The answer to the former is implicit in the previous remarks on the human-ideal character of classicism. In draping themselves in classical guise, the greatness of sovereigns was presented as an echo of Roman imperial dignity. But we should not forget that something more common found simultaneous expression, for the classical orders represent, as we have said, types of human character and corresponding environmental characters. Ideally, these characters are universally applicable, though they required the southern sun-space to emerge as graspable gestalt. This is the background of the northerners' longing for the South, whereas southerners experience no reciprocal draw to the North. But though northern inhabitants feel the lack of southern self-understanding and attempt to bring it home with them, the classical remains always foreign for its eidos requires southern space to become real. Why, then, import the classical when it is of little use? The answer is simple: it is always possible to accommodate the foreign to the domestic so that, though concealed, it can nonetheless seep through the web of domestic form. The history of Nordic Renaissance, baroque, and neoclassic styles is the history of this domestication; and naturally, this process took differing courses in the four Nordic lands.

It is, however, somewhat misleading to speak of a "Nordic renaissance." By the sixteenth century, the Italian Renaissance was already past, and the arts had moved into a phase generally called *mannerism.* As the name suggests, it focused on manners, that is, experiment and invention, rather than ideal form. The Reformation, in tandem with the political and cultural climate after 1500, had weakened if not destroyed belief in a stable and harmonious world, and with it, the concept of ideal beauty introduced by Brunelleschi and formulated by Alberti, replacing it by a new search for expression.[8] This occurs with great intensity in Michelangelo's "tragic" art. But Italian mannerism does not involve a new language of forms; it is, in every respect, based on the classic, but attains its purpose by ambiguous and conflictive rendering. Thus, the anthropomorphic columnar order and natural rustication are placed in opposition to each other, as an expression that mankind is no longer part of a comprehensive whole, but must struggle to achieve understanding.[9] Only at the close of the century did baroque rhetoric-synthetic art manage to cope with this problem.

Italian mannerism's doubt and search, however, is not the origin of Nordic mannerism. Here, we recognize instead an attempt to adapt the classical to the domestic, and the result is a new face for classicism. This adaptation occurred already en route from Italy to the North; the classical in fact arrived in the Nordic lands via Holland and Germany, and was in the first instance stamped by their previous interpretations. In both countries, an attempt had been made to conjoin the domestic and the classical; as a result, half-timbering was divided into small column and beam segments, while gables were reformed as a superposition of stories, with volute transitions. The result was a mobile contour, which despite its Vitruvian elements seems anything but classical; a logical tectonic wall was replaced by an irrational web. In Holland, the original skeletal structure found expression in the extensive use of glass. Columns were moreover transformed into fantastic and ominous monsters, which have little in common with Greek caryatids save that they stand upright in space. Forssman points out that these metamorphoses appear primarily in portal elements, as a symbol for a building's content.[10] In general, we recognize how classical forms become subject to radical domestication on their passage to the North.

Nordic mannerism came to its most convincing expression in Denmark, where its development led to what can truly be called a style. Already in the mid-sixteenth century, several manor houses were built in "Danish Renaissance style," such as Hesselagergaard (completed 1538) and Egeskov (completed 1554), both on Fyn. An echo of medieval brick architecture is still perceptible, but a new will to geometric order is conspicuous: in the symmetrical plan, the accentuate superposition of stories, and the formation of details. A desire for simplification and calm characterizes the whole. Such is the moated Egeskov: it seems a friendly castle of human scale, beautifully expressive of the Danish domestic sense. The Danish Renaissance culminated under Christian IV, and its development can be traced if one compares his lodge Rosenborg (1606–34) with Egeskov.[11] While Egeskov is still a unified volume, Rosenborg is subject to a "net" of horizontal and vertical lines. The ground plan is clearly systematized, and the stories are laid upon one another without interstitial differentiation. A classical tone is struck by numerous triangular window pediments, but with respect to size and formation, they are repeated unvaryingly throughout the whole. An open, abstract form results, essentially anticlassical, neither conclusive nor plastic. What Rosenborg has in common with the Italian Renaissance is only its thorough geometric order; but while this was only implied in Italy, here it is visualized as a half-timbering of light sandstone on red brick surfaces. The complex volutes of the gables, too, are anticlassical; further, the whole is marked by the presence of towers, additively stacked in sections. Rosenborg is thus both Nordic and Danish, and the import has been domesticated.

Egeskov Castle, Fyn, Denmark

Egeskov Castle, Fyn, Denmark

Doorway, von der Lindeska House, Gamla Stan,
Stockholm

It is well known that Christian IV took an active part in the design of his buildings, but he employed many professionals such as the influential family of master builders, the van Steenwinkels from Holland. As a result, the Danish renaissance is often characterized as Dutch, and indeed a certain kinship is unquestionably present. But it must be emphasized that the Danish works have an independent character. The high, narrow gable houses of Holland for instance are replaced by the domestic *længe* (farm building), and the relationship between wall and window is also different. Additionally, the "shimmering" use of material that identifies Dutch architecture finds a new calm in Denmark, and this, no doubt, is a result of the differing relation of the interweaving of land and water in the respective countries. The process of domestication began already under Frederik II, particularly in Frederiksborg palace (bathhouse 1580), while Kronborg (completed 1574) was still impressed by foreign motifs. Additions to Frederiksborg (1602–20), carried out under Christian IV, provided Denmark with the most impressive monument of the period. The style is the same as that of Rosenborg, but its execution is less uniform, and a multiplicity of Nordic details enrich the complex. It is interesting to note that the palace chapel has Gothic windows, confirming that the Renaissance style represents a new world image. The architecture of the epoch culminates with the Stock Exchange (Børsen) in Copenhagen (1619–40, Laurens and Hans van Steenwinkel the Younger). Here, the open and repetitive organization of the plan and facade are executed with extreme consistency; but simultaneously, Nordic mannerism's bizarre detailing pervades, and the domestication of the foreign is thus accomplished.

Christian IV is also known as the founder of a number of new cities.[12] In general his projects were based on Renaissance-ideal plans, whose geometrical spatial organization formed the basis for the repetitive building types that the period favored. Among these city plans, Norway's capital Christiania (1624; now Oslo) is the most significant. Christian IV resolved that the town should be removed to below the walls of Akershus fortress, after the medieval town further east was destroyed by fire. The plan unites prototypical ideal order with pragmatic accommodation to the local topography and therefore deserves to be seen as an "art of planning." Unfortunately, several subsequent fires have reduced the original building stock to a few remains, but the disposition of space remains, reminiscent of the comprehensive vision of the seventeenth century. In Denmark, this comprehensiveness comprises buildings of widely differing types, and though their style was developed in connection with palace buildings, it could equally well be applied to ordinary urban houses and public buildings. This versatility is a result of both its spatial organization and its built form; therefore, the architecture of Christian IV should be designated realistic rather than ideal. In general, this entails a new interpretation of the traditional Danish qualities we outlined in connection with its half-timbered architecture and thereby of the Danish landscape.

Stock Exchange, Copenhagen

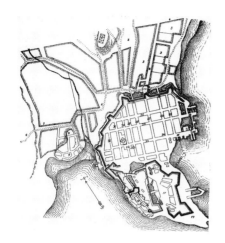

Christian IV's plan for Christiania (Oslo)

Fredriksborg Castle, northeast Zealand, Denmark

Fredriksborg Castle, northeast Zealand, Denmark

Fredriksborg Castle, northeast Zealand, Denmark

In Sweden, the assimilation of the foreign occurred differently; the intention here was not a new interpretation of spatial order but the introduction of new motifs expressive of the world image of the time. This can be clearly seen if one compares the castle at Vadstena (1545–1602) with Rosenborg. Vadstena's disposition as a curtain wall between two towers is not unlike the Danish complex, but it is principally different with respect to configuration. Here, there has been no attempt made to inscribe the building within a geometrical net; rather, the whole remains a collocation of individual volumes of the Swedish type, with characteristic rondels at the corners. The facade seems a continuous ground for applied motifs, and classical motifs appear in connection with portals, windows, and pediments. (Here too, we may note the Gothic windows of the chapel.) The result is a building renown for its "Swedishness." Here is Ragnar Östberg's description (1900):

> The portals stand firmly, clearly, and with conviction, like in southern monumental works, but with a Nordic component of naive power that permeates all and renders it ours. The formation of windows has likewise this springy, original sharpness one wants to call Swedish, and which, in any case, provides a fascinating view of what our Vikings already fought for: the treasures by the Mediterranean Sea. The massive masonry bears these jewels like a mountain does its vegetation. The whole building rises like a bulwark—indeed what it was and still is—a bulwark for the Swedish in us even now, with gravity, playfulness, weight, and refinement. It is the flanking towers and gables that sing out the joy of refinement.[13]

Here, one of Sweden's greatest architects gives a fitting characterization of the essence of Swedish architecture and provides us with a key to understanding the domestication of the classical.

In its symmetrical disposition of clear volumes, Vadstena has assimilated basic classical features that were not yet present in a project such as Gripsholm (completed 1537), in which a picturesque medieval quality is still dominant. Further developments of the classical can be traced in the Tidö castle (completed 1625), Riddarhuset in Stockholm (1641–60), Skokloster (1650–58), and the Drottningholm palace (1662–80). In connection with these works, one encounters the names of many architects: the French Simon de la Vallée, the Dutch Jost Vingboons, and the German Nicodemus Tessin the Elder, indeed, Swedish classical architecture had a more diverse background than the Danish.[14] At Tidö, we encounter a style that would come to identify Swedish classicism and to a certain degree its later Norwegian development: against a ground of neutral continuous wall surfaces, window openings are incised as precise holes, and characteristic details are limited to portal surrounds, frontispieces, and other closures. Here again, motifs appear as reminders rather than as constitutive elements. Contemporary dwellings in Stockholm likewise possessed a corresponding quality.[15]

Vadstena Castle, Sweden

Vadstena Castle, Sweden

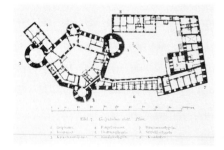

Gripsholm Castle, Sweden, plan

Gripsholm Castle, Sweden

The abstraction here manifest culminated with the Skokloster castle, a dry and theoretical work probably designed by the client himself, General Carl Gustav Wrangel. Nevertheless, Skokloster is a highly characteristic example of the development of Nordic classicism, wherein southern plastic presence dematerializes. In the Riddarhuset of Jost Vingboons, however, we can detect a larger conception and richer articulation. Dutch reminders are lent a domestic tone thanks to Jean de la Vallée's paraphrased Swedish manor house roof. A similar domestication marks the Drottningholm palace, "Sweden's Versailles," by Nicodemus Tessin the Elder. Here and in other works Tessin emerges as an architect of European class, demonstrating a familiarity with contemporary trends. As such, his Federal Bank (Riksbank) in Stockholm (1662–82) echoes Roman palazzo facades, though the building's rise gives it a Nordic tone. Of special interest is the Carolinian crypt (Karolinska gravkoret) of the Riddarholm church (completed 1661), where Tessin takes up ideas from Borromini's St. Ivo in the vertical continuity that joins the lower region and the cupola; it is indeed a masterful work where classical elements engage in a web of horizontal and vertical lines.

Both Drottningholm and the Carolinian crypt are baroque works that lead us toward the work of the period's most significant architect, Nicodemus Tessin the Younger.[16] As the architect of the new palace in Stockholm, Tessin achieved great renown, both home and abroad. After an extended period of study (1673–78) in Rome, under Bernini and Carlo Fontana, he returned to Sweden and quickly received a number of commissions. When the old castle with the triple crown tower burned in 1697, Tessin was chosen as architect for the new building. He was already an experienced professional, having been engaged for several years with additions to the old castle, among other work. From the first, it was Tessin's intention to reinvigorate Swedish architecture. His criticism of Nordic medieval architecture is well known, as well as his conscious desire for the introduction of Bernini's style. His biographer, Ragnar Josephson, describes the architect's intentions in the chapter "Break with Tradition" (Brottet med tradisjonen): "Following the lead of the de la Vallées and his father, Tessin broke down the vertical in Swedish building culture. He waged an attack against high buildings, towers, spires, gables, domes, and steep roofs."[17] Thus Tessin transformed the house from a standing to a lying form, allowing the horizontal to dominate.

The significance of the horizontal in baroque architecture is as an expression of a general desire to conquer the surroundings. By the seventeenth century, the castle was no longer a goal and place of refuge in contrast to the environs but rather a point of departure for a network of radiating axes that manifested the dominant role of the center. This was true of church buildings and especially of palace complexes. Louis XIV's Versailles is prototypical; here, baroque space expresses the period's absolutism. In general, architecture became part of a conscious policy of influence aimed at securing the participation of the governed classes.[18] In this respect, the baroque was

Riddarhuset, Stockholm

Skokloster, Sweden

not just a southern phenomenon, but in that its premise is the representation of omnidirectional homogeneous space, it belongs principally within the classical tradition.[19]

As we remarked, Tessin familiarized himself with the aims of the baroque, more specifically those as interpreted by the school of Bernini. His palace complex in Stockholm thus seems markedly Roman: both its disposition and edifice are inspired by Bernini's project for the Louvre. The basic concept of building as dominant over the environment is clearly expressed; nonetheless, the four facades are differentiated with respect to their situation. The Doric rustication of the outer courtyard corresponds to its service character, while the giant Corinthian order toward the sloping Castle Hill it faces gives this facade the representative quality that befits the main entry to the Hall of State (Rikssalen) and the palace church. The sea front, with projecting side wings, interacts with the natural space without, and its base of stone blocks is reminiscent of the kullar around the Mälar. The fourth facade facing Norrbro is of a larger scale, in response to the plan for a monumental square at Norrmalm. Just as the castle was no longer the goal in the environs, the palace's internal court is not configured as a terminal point, but rather functions as a point of origin for the axes of the facades. Despite its Roman features and its adherence to international baroque ideals, Stockholm's palace is indeed expressive of a certain process of domestication. This can be clearly seen in the absence of true plasticity. The complex has a dry character that is anything but Italian, and classical forms are applied individually, in a Swedish manner, particularly the triumphal arch motif facing the Castle Hill.

N. Tessin, the elder, National Bank, Stockholm

N. Tessin, the elder, Drottningholm Palace, Sweden

These features are reiterated in the house Tessin built for himself facing the palace's main entrance (1692–1700). Fronting the Castle Hill, it seems an abstract version of a Roman palazzo facade. As such, its execution points toward the simplified classicism that later became a common Nordic phenomenon. The internal garden is without doubt Tessin's most imaginative work; its double trapezoidal plan, its freestanding wings, and its enclosing perspective make it a masterpiece of baroque spatial composition, while simultaneously, the formal solution represents accommodation to a tight and difficult site.[20] Josephson says, with good reason, "Intimate enclosure and free range are difficult to link, but are here united. With architectonic and decorative sleights of hand, Tessin has understood how to conquer enforced spatial limitation; the eye seldom encounters a solid wall, but meets

N. Tessin, the younger, Royal Palace, Stockholm

N. Tessin, the younger, Royal Palace, Stockholm

N. Tessin, the younger, Tessinska Palace, Stockholm

N. Tessin, the elder, Karolinska Funerary Chapel, Riddarholm Church, Stockholm

constantly changing, rich views. The architect, with illusionistic device, has broken through the tight frame of the urban site."[21] This description suggests that an echo of Nordic space resounds in Tessin's garden; here, broad baroque gestures have become domestic.

Not surprisingly, we find a rich baroque architecture in Denmark as well. As the second of the North's great powers, Denmark needed also to manifest the objectives of absolutism. While Christian IV's architecture still had clear roots in the country's building tradition, Christian VI and Frederik V's projects seem far more international. They trail Swedish baroque by about fifty years and thus have lighter features that are closer to the rococo. The two leading architects of this period, Lauritz Thura and Nicolai Eigtved, were native Danes and, perhaps as a result of their origins, sought to bring themselves "up to date."[22] For both, a several-year residence in Germany and Italy was of decisive significance, and as a result, their works echo with received impressions—for example Thura's spire on Our Saviour Church (Vor Frelsers Kirke) in Copenhagen, which borrows Borromini's famous helix for St. Ivo in Rome. This very spiral, however, illustrates that the foreign cannot be taken over directly; to an even greater degree than in the work of Tessin, southern plasticity is discarded in favor of a drier geometry. But this is not to suggest that Thura and Eigtved were unable to infuse their work with presence and charm, for indeed their works are characterized by a typical Danish friendliness.

The quality of Danish baroque is clearly evident in the period's major work, Amalienborg Square at Frederiksstaden in Copenhagen (Nicolai Eigtved, 1750–54).[23] As both an urban scheme and a public square, it adheres to the ideals of the time; thus, all facades are of the same type, after the French pattern. They are symmetrically composed, with the prescribed superposition of stories. The square itself is configured after the prototype of the French *place royale,* with an equestrian statue of the king standing at the center of an elementary geometric space, in this case, an octagon. Four similar houses for the nobility were situated at the four diagonals of the octagon.[24] But while the French *place* creates a continuous wall, Eigtved divided the whole in a series of differing, but similarly composed, volumes. In so doing, he made the scale more human, so that the project, which in its main features acts an expression of absolutism, becomes a domestic "place to be." Amalienborg Square is unquestionably one of the period's most pleasant urban spaces, and its quality is extended into the Frederiksstaden streets with their fine combination of continuity and variation. The project as a whole was to have been dominated by a grand domed church on axis with the square, but this, however, was never executed.[25] Despite their domestic traits, Eigtved's buildings do not seem particularly Nordic.

A more directly Danish interpretation of the baroque language characterizes the Fredensborg Palace northwest of Copenhagen (J. C. Krieger,

Amalienborg, Copenhagen

N. Eigtved, Amalienborg, Copenhagen

N. Eigtved, Fredriksstaden, Copenhagen

Fredensborg Castle, Zealand, Denmark

completed 1719). Here, we can see precisely that simplification of the classical that is typical of the Nordic lands; it consists in the negation of the plastic, and in Denmark, in a thoroughly ordered rhythm. Thus we again find that foreign currents can receive endemic interpretation.

We have remarked that the increased significance of royal power played an essential role in the development of architecture in the sixteenth and seventeenth centuries, and we have also noted that the political and social restructuring was linked to the Reformation, with the introduction of Luther's teachings to the Nordic countries. These changes called for a new type of church, where reminders from the Catholic past were effaced and the needs of the new holy service were met. As we know, the word attained central importance. We might also add that the Reformation was the precursor of Enlightenment rationalism, and thus of the desire for a clear, comprehensible architecture. The solution was a unified space of assembly, in which pulpit and altar share equal importance. The path motif of the Early Christian basilica was, in other words, discarded in favor of centralization. The symbolic contrast between above and below was weakened as well, especially with respect to the admittance of light. Similar tendencies occurred during the Italian Renaissance, when uniformly lit centralized churches became the common ideal. This confirms that Protestant church building was not merely functionally conditioned but was moreover an expression of a universal world image in which rational order supplanted mystical participation. In the South, this objective was later abandoned as a result of the Counter Reformation's demand for ecstatic participation, a demand that was met by Bernini's *teatrum sacrum*.[26] The space of the Protestant church, however, also needed to affect psychologically, so as to withstand the attack by the Counter Reformation; as a result, many Nordic interiors from the sixteenth and seventeenth centuries echo catholicism's teatrum.

As a main commission, the church was soon overshadowed by the palace; and since most towns were adequately furnished with church buildings from the Middle Ages, ecclesiastic building became, for the most part, rebuilding. Many Norwegian stave churches, for example, were altered to become cross-plan churches by the addition of wooden transepts, and, at the same time, many were punctured with windows. But a number of medieval churches were demolished and replaced by more timely buildings. Protestant church building yielded some major works, such as Christian IV's Trinity Church (Trefoldighetkirke) at Kristianstad in Skåne (1618–28). In plan, it is a centralized hall in which a series of spatial segments forms a synthesis of rectangle and cross. The slim pillars that bear the gothicized vault create an enchanting effect. This church was echoed in the Trinity Church in Christiania (Oslo) (1632–39, destroyed by fire 1686) and later in Our Savior's Church (Vor Frelsers Kirke) in Copenhagen (Lambert van Haven, 1682; spire by Thura, 1750), where brick construction attained a more unitive, baroque formation through the use of the giant pilaster order. Significant churches were built in Sweden in the sixteenth century as well, such as the domed, centralized Katarina Church in Stockholm (Jean de la Vallée 1656–90; dome by G. J. Adelkrantz, 1723, following a fire) and the cathedral in Kalmar (N. Tessin the elder; completed 1660), which is a baroque aula church with a centralized transept, surrounded by four small towers at the crossing. With the development of the mining towns Kongsberg and Røros, Norway, important churches were built in the eighteenth century.[27]

Of special interest are the numerous wooden churches in Finland and Norway, for these clearly express the domestication of the foreign.[28] Their groundplans are usually centralized, most often Greek cross or octagonal. Typologically, they agree with general Protestant models, while manifesting the world image of a "new epoch."[29] But characteristic local features are also present. In Finland, it was common to place a freestanding belfry on axis in front of the main entry, in the Russian manner. Large unitive roofs echo those of medieval stone churches, and their interiors translate the cavernous effect into complex vault formations that represent a new interpretation of an original Finnish type and a regional manifestation of the period's spatial geometry. Among numerous examples, we can mention the magnificent church in Petäjävesi (Jaakko K. Leppänen 1763–65).

In Norway, too, local features are conspicuous. Here, the tower is enjoined with the building itself, either as a western tower over one of the cross plan's central arms, or as a central tower topping the crossing; the latter is reminiscent of the stave church's centralized verticality. The interiors are less emphatically cavernous than in Finland, but a smaller "heavenly vault" over the crossing is common, whereas octagonal plans generally produce

L. Thura, Our Saviour Church, Copenhagen

Petäjavesi Church, Finland

Hjartdal Church, Telemark, Norway

more complex solutions. Of special interest are a group of cross-plan churches in Telemark in which one arm has been separated from the main space by the insertion of a "pulpit-altar," so that a T-shaped space results. The pulpit-altar originated in Germany and gained favor in Denmark and Sweden before reaching Norway in the eighteenth century; it is formed by placing the pulpit above the altar at the central axis of the space. With the addition of a choir gallery, and possibly an organ, the pulpit-altar became a full wall, which appears as the termination of the space. In this way, the word takes its place at the center.[30]

In general, the history of Nordic Renaissance and baroque is the history of the domestication of the foreign, realizing an architecture that possesses classical validity without thereby adhering to a southern plastic understanding of form. The objective was, in other words, to manifest the universal in a Nordic manner, not by means of a medieval contradiction of the classical language of form but by extracting its basic qualities. The "abstract classicism" that arose approached its final form just after 1800 in works that, despite their affinity to European neoclassicism, reaffirm a domestic tone.

Neoclassicism must be seen in the context of the Enlightenment and its societal consequences. It represented, in the main, a reaction against absolutism and its forms of expression, a wish to return to something original. This objective became linked to the Newtonian subversion of the traditional anthropocentric world image. Alexander Pope's familiar couplet says it thus:

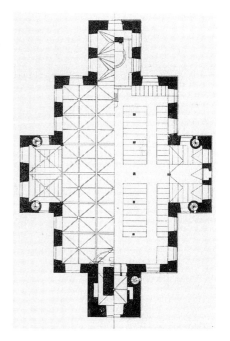

Kristianstad Church, Sweden, plan

> Nature and nature's laws lay hid in night;
> God said, "Let Newton be!," and there was light.

Newton's natural science became associated with the concept of liberty that received its decisive manifestation during the French Revolution. For the Enlightenment, liberty did not entail the eradication of all rules but rather a rediscovery of the ostensibly natural origins of knowledge.[31] It is against this background that we may understand neoclassicism. Its combination of elementary geometries and basic characters resurrects architecture as an autonomous discipline, that is, cleansed of all particular symbols and superficial decoration.[32] Thus neoclassicism retains the classical, but without accepting the more local plastic aspects of the southern understanding of form. (It is, for example, indicative that columnar entasis is omitted.)

Neoclassicism does, however, have roots in this period that it opposes; as we indicated earlier, it developed under the Renaissance and baroque. It should also be added that certain French and English works played a significant part in the development of "abstract classicism." The tendency is visible already in Hawksmoor's churches from the first three decades of the seventeenth century and culminates with the projects of the revolution-

C. F. Hansen, Our Lady Church, Copenhagen

ary French architects Ledoux and Boullée toward the end of the century.[33] Here, architecture has become elemental in that buildings are conceived as assemblages of stereometric volumes, such as the cube, the cylinder, and the tetrahedron; indeed, even the sphere came into use. Walls stand naked, stripped of all organic tactility. In general, it is a sort of international style that lays claim to ubiquitous validity. This objective must be seen in the context of the demographic restructuring of the period and the beginnings of an international urbanism. In general, we can designate the ideals of the period as "purist typology."[34]

In the North, abstract classicism finds unparalleled expression in the work of the Danish architect Christian Frederik Hansen. Among his numerous works in Copenhagen and Slesvig-Holstein, his Church of Our Lady (Vor Frue Kirke) occupies a central position. Copenhagen's cathedral had been destroyed under the English bombardment in September 1807, and C. F. Hansen was quickly engaged for its reconstruction.[35] Because the masonry walls from the destroyed church had to be reused, a basilica with a western tower was prescribed—a plan that originated in the Gothic church built there in 1316. Hansen, however, informed the church with the simplest possible volumetric design, in accordance with the ideals of the time. Nave and aisle, then, were treated as a parallelepiped, and the choir was added as a semidomed half-cylinder. The composition of the west front is similarly elemental, forming a neutral background to the Doric portico, where columns stand without entasis. The interior, too, is Doric, in clear violation of the Vitruvian tradition that prescribes the Ionic for churches dedicated to the Virgin Mary churches. The space has a cool and abstract character that in its timelessness seems to obliterate all regionalism. But despite all ideal intentions, Hansen's work bears a Danish tone. This is confirmed if we see it in context with Denmark's traditional "latent classicism," which reemerged around 1920.

In Norway, the University in Oslo provides the greatest contribution to neoclassicism. While the city's Royal Palace is designed within the limits of a more conventional Palladian style (H. D. F. Linstow 1824–48), the university represents a more advanced solution in which the simplified volumes of the period are linked with a new will to constructive/formal articulation of the facade. It is well known that the architect Christian Heinrich Grosch sent, in 1838, his drawings to Schinkel in Berlin, who undertook essential improvements.[36] The architecture of the facade is thus based on Schinkel's Schauspielhaus, with its combination of small and giant order. Of special interest is the vestibule to the *domus media* with its magnificent open staircase, a variation of Schinkel's solution at the Altes Museum. In general, the university is less abstract than C. F. Hansen's building and represents both a further development of and an accommodation to the Norwegian tradition that laid stress upon the constructive substance of the built work.

C. H. Grosch, University, Christiania (Oslo)

It is legitimate to say that Nordic neoclassicism culminated with the Senate Square in Helsinki. Here, we encounter a unique whole, in that the design of the senate chambers, the university, the library, and the cathedral, grouped around a central square, were entrusted to the same architect. After emancipation from Sweden in 1809, Finland attained the status of a Grand Duchy, under the Russian monarchy. The little town Helsingfors (Helsinki) was chosen to substitute for Åbo (Turku) as the new capital, and a general city plan was developed by J. A. Ehrenström (1810–12).[37] In 1814, the German architect Carl Ludwig Engel was called in to design the new capital's monumental buildings. The project was characteristically expressive of the new society that followed the Enlightenment. The symbolic center here is not the palace but a group of democratic institutions. That the project was designed by one man is, however, unique.

Engel arrived in Helsinki after an extended residency in Tallinn (Reval), St. Petersburg, and Turku, and had received decisive influence from contemporary Russian architecture. It has been noted that he never visited France or Italy, and as a result his background was somewhat one-sided; his buildings have in fact a more picturesque quality than contemporary architecture in Denmark and Norway. Thus, we find neither abstract classicism's naked wall surfaces nor Schinkel-like structural components but rather a richness of motifs that echo St. Petersburg architecture. Of special note is the free use of columns and pilasters in the library (1836–44). Engel's en-

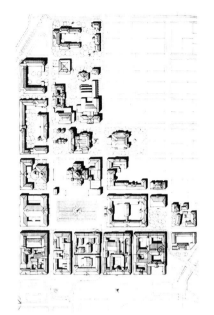

C. L. Engel, Senate Square, Helsinki

View from the Esplanade toward Senate Square

semble was modified somewhat after his death, in that an urban staircase with flanking pavilions was built, and the Nicolai church was furnished with four towers surrounding the central dome. This latter modification was carried out after the wishes of the Czar, who wanted to strengthen the church's Russian appearance.[38]

Our discussion of the assimilation of the classical into the North has shown that the foreign can be given local roots if it is modified in accordance with the local building tradition. That such a domestication was possible was a result of a formal language that, despite its origins under the southern sun, had a universal basis, and is as such, in principle, ubiquitously valid. This basis can be suggested by the key words *spatial order* and *built character*. It is evident, however, that this basis cannot be directly assumed but must instead permeate, so that the individual works may appear as a manifestation of the universal. Christian IV's and C. F. Hansen's Danish architecture illustrate this idea exemplarily. In Sweden, Tessin the Younger succeeded in formulating a Swedish classicism of durable value—indeed, so durable that neoclassicism became unnecessary. In Norway, Grosch, with the help of Schinkel, renewed Norwegian architecture's structural approach and thereby laid the ground for future building. And finally, Engel created a Finnish classicism that appropriately expresses that country's unfinished order. Hence each of the four Nordic lands was successful in lending a voice to the great classical polyphony. The manifold unity thus formed around 1800 was nonetheless unable to continue indefinitely because of the unsatisfied need for identity.[39] For during the nineteenth century, it was precisely the representation and definition of national identity that overshadowed all else.

L. Sonck, Telephone Association, Helsinki

In the mid-1900s, a new wooden architecture became common whose identifying features were broad verandas in several stories, large windows, wide eaves, and richly ornamented gables and parapets. This style spread incredibly quickly from Scandinavia to Italy, from Russia to France—indeed, even in the United States it made an impact on the surroundings.[1] It is evident that a "new age" sought to find an appropriate form of expression. The style was employed primarily in connection with suburban dwellings but some larger buildings, such as restaurants, hotels, and sanatoriums were also executed similarly. In every case, there is an evident desire for contact with nature.

In Europe, the new wooden architecture came to be known as the *Swiss style.* Its point of reference was doubtless Switzerland's characteristic folk architecture, rather than its urban building, for the Swiss farmhouse exhibits exactly the features mentioned above. Thus for the first time, folk architecture was taken as the model for an international style.[2] How is it, then, that nineteenth-century society, so based in industrialization and urbanization, chose as a model a folk typology?

Before we answer this question, it is important to point out that this new architecture was not a replication of its Swiss prototype. Neither the chalet of the Alps nor the farmhouses of Emmental and Simmental were imitated directly, that is, as gestalt; the Swiss traits consisted instead in a formal and constructive vocabulary that could be assembled in various ways and accommodate the character of a foreign place. Indeed, the style manifested itself differently from country to country, though its basic features remained. The reference to Swiss typology was thus of a general nature. Significantly, the Swiss style was linked to programs that were a result of new conditions, that is, programs with democratic presuppositions. It is easy to understand why liberation was sought from the prototypes of church and palace, to instead introduce an architecture with roots in daily life. But the open world that was forming did not contradict the wish for national and domestic identity; in fact, the French revolution had cleared the way with a concept of freedom that had national identity as one of its aims. It is in precisely this context that Switzerland became a natural model. As Europe's first democratic nation, it was regarded as an ideal in the nineteenth century, for here, all citizens took part in the country's government, and the contribution and significance of the individual was manifest in a folk architecture that, by means of the qualities mentioned above, expressed this new freedom.[3] Swiss architecture resonated convincingly with the country's nature and thereby became a symbol of national identity.[4] As a result, the Swiss style came to play a significant part in the open world of the nineteenth century, although it did not directly express its increasing industrialization.

Against this background, we may look more closely at the qualities that distinguish the Swiss style. Its constructive origins lay in a skeletal structure that may be present throughout the building, or only in certain

Kviknes Hotel, Sogn, Norway

parts, such as gables and verandas. The structure is essentially anticlassical and related to Gothic. Vincent Scully thus characterizes its American variant as the "stick or shingle style," that is, "an architecture based on the dynamic of interwoven elements, rather than the stasis of cubic mass."[5] Here again we encounter the Nordic web and can see that the new open society has a deep affinity to the Nordic world, in contrast to the "complete" world of the South. Stick construction implies a new freedom with respect to the disposition of spaces in that it makes possible larger openings, enhanced contact between inside and out, and freer plan configurations. Additionally, the skeleton can be worked out in the details so as to emphasize the basic qualities of the system; color, too, came into use as a means of stressing built form. Toward the end of the century, however, houses were commonly painted white, and thereby the skeletal structure was veiled, but in return they gained the light, summery character that reaffirmed the new freedom.

The primary skeleton was often filled in with fretsaw ornamentation, reminiscent of Gothic tracery. Because these ornaments were factory produced and available by catalog, they were affordable and showed that democracy, in principle, made goods accessible to all. The ornaments consisted of geometric, vegetal, and zoomorphic motifs; especially popular was the decoration of the gable with a rising sun, aurora. But it was the large windows and verandas that were the style's distinguishing features; the new world's freedom is expressed and kinship to the iron-and-glass architecture of the period is evident through them. Generous fenestration also acted as a sign of better living standards, suggesting spacious and light rooms within. In fact, Norwegian physicians recommended Swiss-style houses as being healthier than the dark dwellings of the past.[6] The gables and eaves, as archetypical signs of the house, met the needs of a residential architecture with original roots. It should be noted that while classicism sought to recover original character, the Swiss style was concerned with originality as an aspect of the inhabitant's "being in space," and thereby anticipates modern architecture. Again Vincent Scully: "Behind the whole development of free design stood the conviction that man must live as a free individual in close contact with nature in order to realize his possibilities."[7]

H. D. F. Linstow, guard house, Royal Palace, Christiania (Oslo)

H. M. Schirmer, Villa Fridheim, Krødsherad, Norway

The introduction of the Swiss style in the Nordic countries occurred gradually and by various routes, but it is natural to emphasize the role played by Christiania's palace architect, H. D. F. Linstow. Linstow devoted much of his time to the design of small wooden houses and journeyed to Germany to study the new wooden architecture there. During his visit, he met Schinkel in Berlin and admired the German architect's constructive honesty, "especially when he works with wood." After returning home to Norway, Linstow built several wooden houses in and around the palace park (Slottsparken) in Christiania, including his own house (1839–1848). In these works we can see the features of the new style fully developed: skeletal structure, large windows, and covered verandas with infill ornamentation. In an article written shortly after his visit to Germany, he describes these features, emphasizing their kinship to traditional Norwegian typologies, and at the same time criticizing wooden architecture that imitates the masonry forms of the Empire style.

It is important to view Linstow's contribution in the light of the general situation in Norway. After 1800, the living conditions were radically transformed. Concurrent with the introduction of new methods of production in farming, the population increased sharply, and better means of communication linked the far reaches of the country. Political independence from Denmark in 1814 and the new democratic constitution played decisive roles.[8] And though Norway had not achieved full independence, associated as it was with Sweden under a common king, these new conditions made for a strong sense of national identity and thereby created a desire for manifestation of the domestic. This in turn supported a new blossoming in all fields of art.[9] There was, as such, a predilection for the Swiss style, which was already anticipated in development of Norwegian wooden architecture before 1800.

Linstow's pioneering contribution was carried on by his assistants C. H. Grosch and H. E. Schirmer, and by 1850 the Swiss style was fully established. Innumerable dwellings and farmhouses were built or rebuilt in the new manner; indeed, Norwegian railway stations were erected in this style, thereby contributing to its spread. Even today, Swiss-style houses mark the Norwegian landscape. Around the same time, the style began to play a large role in Finland and Sweden, too. There, however, it was linked to summer residences for the well-to-do, while country buildings retained their domestic building tradition.[10] Swiss-style motifs were often added in the Swedish manner, that is, without a direct relation to the structural and formal substance. In general, the employment of the style confirms its expression of the new freedom, both personal and political.

It may seem paradoxical that the Swiss style was linked to manifestations of national character. But we have already pointed out that its employment was not based on direct borrowing of a foreign gestalt as such, but rather on the possibilities inherent in its built form, which could satisfy the current requirements for a more open architecture with roots in everyday life. Its further development, then, was less a reaction to the Swiss style than a utilization of its potential, and this occurs above all through more direct use of domestic motifs.

The desire for a more evident process of domestication has to be seen in the context of the movement for Scandinavian unity that came to play a significant cultural role during the century's second half. In 1856, a large student meeting was held in Uppsala, with hundreds of participants from the universities of Christiania, Copenhagen, Lund, and Uppsala.[11] Many well-known personalities participated, among them Bjørnstjerne Bjørnson, who, inspired by the experience, wrote the national-romantic tale "Synnøve Solbakken" shortly after returning home. In Uppsala, the common Nordic roots of the Scandinavian lands were affirmed, and the desire for their reification. As such, the need for national identity sprang from a common source; the movement to which the meeting lent its support was dubbed Scandinavism.[12]

Inspiration for an architecture more unmistakably Nordic was found in old Norwegian wooden architecture, in particular the stave church. At the World Exhibition in Paris in 1867, Sweden and Norway were represented by a pavilion in the stave church style, and at the corresponding exhibition in 1878, Norway appeared with a pavilion in the form of a loft (*Stabbur*). Still, the Swiss style acted as a referent with respect to skeletal structure and the disposition of spaces, but old Norwegian motifs effected an entirely different character. It was called *dragon style* (*dragestil*), a name that alludes to the dragon heads adorning the gables of stave churches. In Sweden, an *early Nordic* (fornnordisk) style emerged; already in the 1870s, the Swedish doctor Carl Curman built several Nordic houses in Lysekil, after a study tour in Norway in the 1850s.[13] For despite the Swedes' traditional condescending attitude toward its "brother folk," Norwegian influence was strongly felt.

In Norway, the leading exponent of the dragon style was Holm Munthe, who developed the domestic idiom in numerous buildings. Unfortunately, his most significant buildings have been lost to fire, but they are nonetheless preserved in *Die Holzbaukunst Norwegens,* published in Berlin as a joint effort of Munthe and Lorentz Dietrichson in 1893. Included is the hunting lodge Rominten, built by Munthe for Kaiser Wilhelm II east of Berlin in 1891; this work brought the dragon style to Germany, thus closing its developmental circle. Fortunately, one of Munthe's most characteristic works, Frognerseteren in Oslo (1890), is still extant. Though there have been some alterations, the building retains a clear image of the dragon-style formal language. Nearby, there stands a large complex in the same style, Holmenkollen Park Hotell by Balthasar Lange (1892–96, originally built as a sanatorium), which, with its fantastic features signals a new interpretation of the basic character of the Norwegian building tradition.

H. Munthe, Frognerseteren, Christiania (Oslo)

H. Bull, Historical Museum, Oslo

B. Lange, Holmenkollen Park Hotel, Oslo

H. Bull, Historical Museum, Oslo

The dragon style came to a culmination in the work of Henrik Bull, who informed it with art nouveau inspiration, as in his prize-winning dining hall at the World Exhibition of 1900 in Paris.[14] At this time, however, there began a process of differentiation of the common Nordic qualities into separate national styles, and Norway's emancipation from Sweden in 1905 spurred the desire for a purer Norwegian architecture and resulted in the call to liberate the capital city's monumental buildings from the reigning nineteenth-century historicism. As a result, Bull realized a convincing synthesis of art nouveau and domestic motifs in his National Theater (1890–99), Historical Museum (1897–1902), and Government Building (Regjerings Bygningen) (1899–1906).[15]

Before we leave these nineteenth-century endeavors to establish a domestic architecture, we should mention an especially charming and significant contribution to the development of the modern dwelling, the painter Carl Larsson's Lilla Hyttnäs, in Sundborn outside of Falun, in Sweden. Together with his wife Karin, he began building a house in 1883 where site, architecture, and decoration constitute a whole, typical of the period of the *Gesamtkunstwerk*. The desire to give each space an appropriate character was decisive in the design, and since everything from furniture to textiles and decoration was designed in collaboration by the two artists, the result was simultaneously unified and variate. There is a beautiful contrast between the rich, though dark, coloration of the introspective dining room, which might be best characterized as warm, and the living room, which has been called a "Gustavian sunshine room," which represents the quality of Nordic summer light. In the upper story is the painter's highly original bedroom, where the bed is placed centrally, surrounded by bookcases and mood-creating decoration.[16] Karin's bedroom is characterized, conversely, by friendliness and happiness. Finally, there is the library, a sanctum where one finds "calm freedom and great solemnity," to quote Larsson himself. In general, Larsson's house is expressive of the Nordic desire for a home in contact with nature, and today it is visited by many who hope to equal the achievement.[17]

After 1900, several important Swedish architects worked toward the development of a more authentic national style. Among them was Lars Israel Wahlman, whose own house Tallom (1904), near Stockholm, united early Nordic echoes with the gestalt of the Swedish loft. The expressive laying log construction rests upon a base of large stone blocks, in an effective contrast to the cantilevered galleries.[18] With his Engelbrekt Church in Stockholm (1906–14), Wahlman realized Scandinavia's most important art nouveau work. The building rises dramatically from a cliff on the city's northern periphery. The architect has masterfully interpreted the rising movement of the site in a series of stone terraces that continue into the church's more precise volumes, which in turn are gathered as a dominant nave crowned

C. Larson, "Lilla Hyttnäs," Sundborn, Sweden

L. I. Wahlman, Engebrekt Church, Stockholm

C. Larson, "Lilla Hyttnäs," Sundborn, Sweden

L. I. Wahlman, "Tallom," near Stockholm

with a gambrel roof. The tall tower represents a new interpretation of the typical Swedish motif, and both interior and exterior are marked by a rich, eclectic collection of motifs. According to the architect, the church was intended to be a Nordic vision of the Sermon on the Mount.

In Göteborg, we find another church that stands as a Nordic interpretation of the universal, the Masthugg Church by Sigfrid Ericson (1910–12). As does the Engelbrekt Church, it rises upon a cliff, and its edifice is equally powerful. But here, the forms are simpler, and the thickness of the tower more traditional. The interior is of special interest in that it is configured as a cave of wood over a massive lower story of masonry. The effect is strong, elementary: the space ranks unquestionably among the most convincing of the newer interpretations of the Nordic sacred interior.

The markedly Swedish character of the Masthugg Church demonstrates that national architecture had reached a new phase, whose important representatives would be Carl Westman and Ragnar Östberg. In 1903, Westman used the gambrel gable for the first time, and his major work, the Stockholm Court House (*Radhus*) (1909–15) took as its prototype the Vadstena castle, its continuous masonry walls extending from both sides of a strong central tower. The project was hailed as a national monument. As late as 1940, Gustav Näsström could write: "All is become Swedish in material and form: granite, limestone and brick, pine and oak, iron and copper, wool and linen, substantial and muscular, strong and worthy."[19]

Westman's Court House was overshadowed, however, by Östberg's City Hall (Stadshus) (1907–23). Here, Swedishness is softened and enriched by numerous reminders that call to mind inspirations from far beyond the

S. Ericson, Masthugg Church, Göteborg

R. Østberg, City Hall, Stockholm

country's borders. That which in the Court House approaches resemblance, here becomes fairytale-like interpretation, not only of motifs but of locality and contemporary currents as well. Its beautiful situation at the corner of Kungsholmen, right opposite the Old Town (Gamla Stan), required a building that united magnificence with charm. Östberg's tower shows that such a coupling is possible. At the same time it is Swedish in its combination of solid volume and contrasting encrownment, while the volume's curvature lends the whole a new elegance. Something Venetian also seems to resonate, and this is appropriate to the site as well as to Stockholm's renown as the "Venice of the North." The facade facing the lake has a character reminiscent of the Palazzo Ducale, and its detailing takes up the ply of water and reflection. The inner courtyard extends and dematerializes classical motifs in a characteristically Nordic manner. The interior lives up to the expectations the exterior awakes and may be described as a fairytale world of remembrance. It is therefore not surprising that during the functionalist period the Stockholm City Hall was considered romanticism's most "dangerous" manifestation. Incidentally, we can note that Östberg also considered Vadstena a source of inspiration, remarking on, in his description of the palace, the unity of the foreign and the domestic.[20]

Architecture in Denmark after 1900 is similarly distinguished by the tendency to manifest national identity, in contrast to the nineteenth century's superficial mixture of styles. The leader of these national endeavors was Martin Nyrop, who won the competition for the City Hall (Rådhus) in Copenhagen in 1880 (built 1892–1905). Nyrop's first sketch gives valuable insight into his method of work, indeed, what the design of a building in general entails. On one page, he drew a simplified plan, two sections, two somewhat detailed elevations, a volumetric perspective, and a fully detailed window, demonstrating that the creation of architecture consists in the alternation between the whole and the parts, within a total vision. In Nyrop's case, the aim was a building at once monumental and informal, representative and for the people; it fulfills its aim in that it is a strong gestalt of domestic materials. Today, his City Hall seems a little old-fashioned, but one hundred years ago it represented an epochal break with the reigning international historicism.

An authentic modern Danish architecture was most convincingly manifested in the Grundtvig Church, with accompanying housing, by Peder Vilhelm Jensen Klint. The project dates from 1914, but was not completed until 1940.[21] The Danish tradition of building is palpable; in fact, both spatial organization and built form are based on the repetitive geometry that had identified Danish architecture since the Middle Ages. The gestalt, too, builds on Danish prototypes, most conspicuously in the church's stepped gables. Nonetheless, the complex does not seem imitative because Klint has extracted the essence from these traditions, not by means of abstraction à la

C. Westman, Court House, Stockholm

M. Nyrop, City Hall, Copenhagen

P. V. J. Klint, Grundtvig Church, Copenhagen

F. Konow Lund, House, Fantoftveien, Bergen

A. Arneberg and M. Poulsson, City Hall, Oslo

C. F. Hansen but by an articulation and detailing that create a timeless presence, at the same time as the brick unites all the parts. The Grundtvig Complex thus embodies Mies van der Rohe's dictum that "architecture begins when one lays two bricks carefully upon one another." The church's interior represents a high point of essential architecture; here, the message of the Gothic cathedral is universalized in a space that informs us that "that which is has always been."[22] Seldom, perhaps never, has the Nordic world been interpreted with more sublimity, and this is perhaps why Klint's work represents a culmination rather than a new beginning.

In Norway, on the contrary, culmination was both meaningless and impossible. After national independence in 1905, the issue was instead a search for a new point of departure, which needed to be realistic rather than romantic. There could thus be no continuation of the dragon style, because it was inappropriate to modern society, even though in its inceptions it had participated in creating national identity. Now, the matter at hand was the realization of new housing, and as a result, everyday architecture gained a new emphasis. Between 1908 and 1913, Magnus Poulsson designed Norwegian houses for farmers and workers, while his later partner, Arnstein Arneberg, developed a domestic style in connection with larger complexes. Both were educated in Sweden and had experienced their brother folk's search for "Swedishness." It was therefore natural that they attempted to achieve something similar in Norway. Their endeavors culminated in the competition for the City Hall (Radhus) in Christiania (Oslo) in 1915–17, where both Nyrop and Östberg sat on the jury. It took time, however, to realize the project, so that when it was finally built after 1930, new ideas were involved.[23] In general, Arneberg and Poulsson's work represents a transitional period, resulting in no clarification à la Klint. The Norwegian search for a regional foothold came to its perhaps most beautiful expression in the characteristic Bergen architecture from the first three decades of the century. Here, as well, dwellings were of central interest; in the houses of Frederik Konow Lund, the nature of the Vestland found a counterpoint in free lively compositions that remain among the best in Norwegian architecture.

Surprisingly enough, it was in Finland that the search for Nordic identity had its most fruitful results—surprising because Finland's tradition of building was less distinct than that of its neighbors', as a result of its difficult history. But the Finns were fortunate in that they possessed a source of inspiration of such remarkable quality as the *Kalevala*. We have noted that the *Kalevala* comprises a complete cosmology and mythology that explains the character of the country through poetic images. When the Finns needed to manifest their roots, the result was therefore an explosion of creative work.

The first buildings that initiate a national Finnish architecture date from the 1890s. Their precursor was the old timber architecture; thus the large timber house built by the painter Akseli Gallén-Kallela for himself in Ruovesi in 1894 reinterprets the Finnish "cave of wood." The architect Lars Sonck also chose timber as the material for his summer house in Hjörösund on Åland (1895) and further developed this material theme in his house for Sibelius, "Ainola," north of Helsinki, with a touch of Jugendstil. But in Finland, stone is always close at hand: the entire country consists of a solid granite basis, which here and there breaks through the topsoil in low crags. The will to create a durable expression of the surroundings made it natural that stone was employed as a building material. This tendency, however, was not unique to Finland, but was instead an international trend that found credence in all of the Nordic countries.[24] One of the most original exponents of the new stone architecture was the American H. H. Richardson; Swedish and Finnish architects traveled across the Atlantic at the end of the nineteenth century to cull inspiration from his work. But the creation of a stone architecture in countries where wood was the traditional building material was no easy task, and it was only in Finland that these experiments were fully successful.

It is characteristic of the Finnish situation in general that the first example of a genuine national architecture was the National Museum (Kansallismuseo) in Helsinki. An architectural competition was announced in 1900, and the winning project, by Herman Gesellius, Armas Lindgren, and Eliel Saarinen, is an essay in stone in which three Finnish motifs constitute the basic elements: a steep church gable ornamented in the Baltic manner, a round corner tower, and a "belfry" (final project 1902, dedicated 1912). A series of secondary motifs also refer to the Finnish past, and the result is a building of unmistakable national character. While the museum was under design and construction, the three architects built for themselves houses with studios near Lake Vitträsk, west of Helsinki (1902–08). Hvitträsk, as the grouping is called, consists of several units, forming a lively whole.[25] A

L. Sonck, Telephone Association, Helsinki

base story of stone seems to grow out of the granite ground, carrying a series of timbered volumes, partly shingled. Typical Finnish motifs are present, such as the compressed lancet arch and timbered gallery. The character of the interiors varies in response to function, as in Saarinen's timber hall, vaulted and cavernous dining room, and light-filled bedroom, where a variation of Jugendstil has been assimilated. Here, as in the houses of Larsson and Wahlman, the home is the prominent vision.

In general, the work of Gesellius, Lindgren, and Saarinen represents a Finnish interpretation of the international art nouveau, as is well demonstrated by the magnificent Railway Station (Rautatieasema) in Helsinki (1904–14), in which influences from middle European Jugendstil prevails. It is thus interesting to note that Saarinen met Olbrich and Behrens in 1907.[26] In 1923, Saarinen left Finland to live in the United States. His American work is not without interest, but it shows as well the difficulties facing an architect with strong national roots working on foreign soil.

National Finnish architecture culminates in the work of Lars Sonck.[27] Here, there is a successful expression of the domestic world in the

E. Saarinen, Railway Station, Helsinki

E. Saarinen, own house, Hvitträsk, outside of Helsinki

L. Sonck, Cathedral, Tampere, Finland

E. Saarinen, H. Gesellius, and A. Lindgren, National Museum, Helsinki

material of stone. Already in his St. Michael's Church (Mikaelinkirkko) in Turku (Åbo) (competition 1894, built 1899–1905), Sonck shows a remarkable ability to give stone vital expression, an aim that was furthered in his magnificent St. John's Cathedral (Johanneksenkirkko) in Tampere (Tammerfors) (competition 1899–1900, built 1902–07). As in its contemporary, the National Museum, Finnish motifs constitute the elements of the composition; in the beautiful hall, enclosed by an embrasive rib vault, the cave motif finds its most striking formation. Additionally, the detailing of the exterior is masterfully handled, resulting in a whole that is the culmination of stone architecture of the period. Sonck's desire to vitalize masonry comes to a head in his building for the Telephone Association (Puhelinyhdistys) in Helsinki (preliminary design 1903, built 1904–05). Its facade gives permanent form to the anticlassical contents of the Finno-Nordic world through an articulation that infuses heaviness and solidity with mythic, vibratory life. As such, the building confirms that the national can be preserved despite changes in building method. Already in 1907, however, Sonck began to move toward a more subdued language of form, with a resonant classical tone, such as the Mortgage Association Building (Hypoteekkiyhdistys) in Helsinki (1908–09), which appears like a synthesis of the domestic and the foreign.

At some point near the beginning of World War I, architects in the Nordic countries began to lose sight of the way ahead. Both Östberg and Klint had concluded a phase, Arneberg and Poulsson laid no foundation for the future, and Saarinen and Sonck's intentions were in need of reinterpretation. A corresponding situation arose in other European countries as well, where the various modes of art nouveau had played themselves out by 1914.[28] The crisis became acute after the war, when the prevailing conditions proscribed romantic forms of any kind. The result was a new wave of classicism, which we will call *late classicism* in order to distinguish it from the neoclassicism of the nineteenth century. It may seem strange that a return to classicism could be seen to resolve the problems of the time, but let us remember that classicism was the only known international language of form, and hence satisfied the need for something universally applicable. Additionally, classicism already held a firm position in the majority of countries.

But the break with the national did not occur without resistance. In Norway, for example, a number of artists and cultural personalities protested against the "loan from outside." Thus the painter Henrik Sørensen wrote: "Norwegians, as far back as we can remember, have loved colors, instability, movement and generous forms." The classicist Gudolf Blakstad answered the charge in these words: "It is clear that Greeks and Italians, in their great epochs, discovered a whole series of things, we must admit, that nobody in Telemark had even thought of."[29] He pointed out, with his partner Herman

Munthe-Kaas, that a classical tradition existed in Norway as well, and cited Paul Melbes's book, *Um 1800,* because it contains some Norwegian examples. In general, the classicists attempted to give architecture an objective basis, which could replace national romanticism's "tilted head method."[30]

It is not unexpected that late classicism found its first significant manifestation in Denmark, where a potential classicism had always been present. The first work to be considered is the Fåborg Museum by Carl Petersen (1912–15), where classicism emerges as a timeless archetypical gestalt, with respect to both form and space. A certain timidity links the museum to the best in the Danish tradition, while at the same time it adapts to the environment of a small city. The influence of C. F. Hansen is evident, but the whole gets a touch of warmth that the old master's work lacks. As such, Stein Eiler Rasmussen remarked: "Carl Petersen was no grey classicist. He wanted clarity and richness of color."[31] Carl Petersen's pioneer contribution was carried on in a series of significant works, such as Copenhagen's Police Building (Politgård) (1918–24) by Hack Kampmann, with his sons Christian and Hans Jørgen, and in collaboration with Aage Rafn. Here again, we find essential classicism; the round courtyard of the large complex is a consummate piece of architecture. Consistent rhythms mark the whole, giving it a typically Danish tone. Danish late classicism resulted as well in a group of large housing projects, among which the Hornbaek House in Copenhagen (1923) by Kay Fisker is especially characteristic. The full-block building is marked by the repetition of a single type of window more than two thousand times. Nevertheless, the neat detailing and good execution secure a domestic quality.

In Sweden, too, late classicism appeared early on the scene. The first and already significant work is Stockholm's Enskilda Bank by Ivar Tengbom (1912–15). Here, we find all of abstract classicism's distinguishing features: continuous wall surfaces wherein windows lie flush, emblematic columns that bear no architrave, keystones that correspond to no arch, and projecting cornices that rob the building of all plastic effect. The result is a refined, surrealistic expression that usurps the defined characters of Vitruvianism.[32] As such, the building is an authentic Nordic work that suggests that the domestication of classicism still offers many possibilities. Tengbom confirmed this in his major work, Stockholm's Concert House (Konserthus) (1920–26). It is a freestanding, somewhat elongated cube, penetrated by numerous small windows without surround; its blue color emphasizes the dematerialized character, which is also emphasized by the front's endless row of slender columns. In the competition entry, these were Doric, but they were built as Corinthian. The change enhances the building's surreal sense. Assymetrically placed before the facade, the floating figures of Carl Milles's Orpheus fountain provide a significant counterpoint. The interior, before

L. Sonck, Mortgage Association, Helsinki

C. Petersen, Fåborg Museum, Fyn, Denmark

H. Kampmann, Police Building, Copenhagen

I. Tengbom, Enskilda Bank, Stockholm

I. Tengbom, Concert House, Stockholm

alterations in 1971–73, was a simple rectangular volume surrounded by two rows of galleries on three sides. A series of remarkably slender columns encompassed the hall, whose airy atmosphere gave the impression of an exterior rather than an interior, accommodating music, the most abstract of arts.

A sensitive and surreal classicism is also characteristic of Gunnar Asplund's early work.[33] After some introductory studies, we see his style fully developed in Villa Snellman in Djursholm (1917–18). The simple building is given a fantastic character by the application of a multiplicity of "reminders": windows that lead our thoughts toward the eighteenth and nineteenth centuries; classical garlands; a tentlike Gustavian entry baldachin; a pair of Mediterranean shutters; symmetries and asymmetries, and so forth. Here, classicism has truly become an art of moods. Success in this method, however, requires unusual gifts, and Asplund's followers have never reached a corresponding level. The Lister Courthouse (Listers Tinghus) in Sölvesborg (1919–21) belongs to the same mystical world, uniting monumental-public features with popular reminders. Asplund's late classical work culminates with the City Library (Stadbiblioteket) in Stockholm (1921–27). The preliminary project is akin to Tengbom's concert hall, but its execution rendered it radically simplified, resulting in a work of elemental, archetypal value. It is important to note that its abstraction never upsets the building's down/up relation, even though the volumes are totally pure. The rising toward the great rotunda is an essential factor in the composition, and it is tempting to consider that the intention is the expression of mankind's way toward eternal wisdom, which is represented by the circle's perfect form. As such, the round reading room appears as a sort of secularized sanctorum. In general, Tengbom and Asplund succeeded in realizing a genuine Swedish classicism, and thereby completed the domestication that was arrested in Tessin's time.

G. Asplund, City Library, Stockholm

J. Sirén, Parliament, Helsinki

G. Asplund, Villa Snellman, near Stockholm

In Norway, late classicism appeared in 1919 in Blakstad and Dunker's winning project for the New Theater (Det Nye Teater) in Oslo, which was later realized in modern guise. The Haugesund City Hall (Rådhus), on the other hand, was built in accordance with Blakstad and Munthe-Kaas's design from 1922. The building, executed between 1924 and 1931, is late classicism's most important work in Norway and in contrast with the previously mentioned Danish and Swedish works, it has an authentic Norwegian character, which consists in the accentuation of structural substance, appearing in the strong rustication of the base, and the paired columns that lend dignity to the city council chamber. Here, however, it is not a matter of formal abstraction, of the expression of statics, which heightens the contrast between the horizontal extension of the office wing and the vertical rising of the council chamber. Nonetheless, the whole lacks southern plasticity and thus represents a Nordic domestication. The same can be said of the Vigeland Museum in Oslo by Lorentz Harboe Ree and J. Buch (1920–24), which appears more Danish, however, as a result of its delicate detailing.

Among late classicism's other manifestations in Norway, Harald Hals's urban plans and housing project deserve mention. During the twenties, he acted as city planning chief for Oslo and planned a series of urban districts that combine spatial sensitivity with simple and meaningful classical forms.[34] Also of interest is his garden city Ullevål Haveby (1916–21). Here, housing retains a romantic character that seems both English and Norwegian, while the central Dam square introduces classical motifs. The evident intention was the differentiation of the private-domestic from the public-universal, and the result is undoubtedly successful.

It might seem surprising that late classicism came to play as large a role as it did in Finland, but we must keep in mind that Finnish tradition also included classical city plans of the nineteenth century that, despite their Russian flavor, are characterized by strong order.[35] An analogous regularity was again taken up in the 1920s and yielded fine results. Of special interest is the charming garden city Käpylä (Kottby) in Helsinki by Martti Välikangas (1920–25). The complex consists of freestanding wooden houses for one, two, or four families, where the use of classical motifs reveal how little is necessary to raise building to an art. Finnish late classicism culminates with the Parliament in Helsinki by J. S. Sirén (1924–30). Here again there are echoes of Tengbom's concert hall, but the material is now Finnish granite, and the result is an imposing building marked by a certain hardness. Incidentally, it is interesting to note that Finland's great modern architect Alvar Aalto also began as a classicist; between 1919 and 1928, he built several late classical works, among which is the fine Workers Association in his home town Jyväskylä (1925).[36] Here, classicism is consciously undermined: a large closed volume rests upon stout Doric columns, a solution that echoes Peruzzi's mannerist Palazzo Massimo in Rome (1532). Large glass areas on the ground floor, however, signal the coming of modernism.

G. Blakstad and H. Munthe-Kaas, City Hall,
Haugesund, Norway

H. Hals, Ullevål Haveby, Oslo

A. Aalto, Worker's Association, Jyväskylä, Finland

Our discussion of the Nordic endeavors to find their own forms of expression reveals that the national gains meaning only insofar as it forms a part of an international context; and such a context is always present, because any authentic work has a "basic language" of form as its foundation. Classicism manifests this basic language in an especially direct manner. But we have seen that this language can be obscured and contradicted, or even misunderstood and forgotten.[37] When this occurs, a certain unease arises and with it a desire to represent anew "what people in Telemark never even thought of." The result is an alternation between domestication and classical renaissances. For that which is called national romanticism entails precisely this desire for contact with the immediately given, both as mood, and as history. Thus the South knows no real romanticism. There the classical has its origins and requires no domestication; instead, the immediate comes to expression in baroque periods.

The Nordic alternation between romantic and classic phases is not, however, absolute; the romantic has always, and indeed must have, a classical undertone, while classicism is always an object of romantic domestication. It is therefore meaningful to speak of "romantic classicism."[38] It is just such a synthesis of the foreign and the domestic that is of interest in the North. As we have seen, this synthesis was achieved in the Middle Ages by means of contradiction, during the renaissance and baroque periods through vitalization, under neoclassicism by abstraction, and during national romanticism with the help of reminders. The works that made these syntheses manifest rank as the art of building.

Both national romanticism and late classicism were primarily concerned with the language of forms, even though they also took up the issue of a new dwelling. After World War I, this question came to the fore and supported a new objectivity based in the idea that form follows function rather than preestablished building methods, whether foreign or domestic. It might seem that the conflict between the national and the classical had been resolved, once and for all.

A. Aalto, Turun Sanomat, Turku, Finland

The slogan "form follows function" pretends to be universally applicable, and since our world is becoming increasingly characterized by global sameness, the inevitable result is an international architecture. The desire for the international was indeed a dominant tendency in the twenties, and for the first time architecture lost its regional and local traits. We are all familiar with functionalism's formal expressions: elemental, white building volumes, flat roofs, strip windows, minimal detailing—in other words, an architecture wherein all that is special has been cut away, so that only the naked, abstract form remains. Such are the buildings of the thirties of such architects as Markelius and Bryggman, Lassen and Korsmo.

The tendency for an international architecture was intentional. It was already apparent in the first Bauhaus book from 1925, in which Walter Gropius collected "moderne baukunst" from many countries under the title *International Architecture.*[1] Gropius used "world commerce" and "world technology" (Weltverkehr and Welttechnik) as the basis for the choice of the material and the title. In 1931, the Museum of Modern Art in New York held its first architectural exhibition; again, the title is symptomatic: The International Style. The introduction of the word *style* underscored that the new architecture had a definite aesthetic basis: "The idea of style as the frame for potential growth, rather than a fixed and crushing mould, has developed with recognition of underlying principles," states the book that followed in the wake of the exhibition, which emphasized "structure" and "function" as defining factors.[2]

It is well known that modern architecture and art sought to discover underlying principles. "It must recover the most primitive things, as though nothing had ever been done before," wrote S. Giedion, meaning that it was a matter of finding the origin, or that which had been obscured with the nineteenth century's use of superficial historic motifs.[3] Similar pronouncements from the pioneers of the movement are legion.[4]

The first systematic attempt toward the formulation of basic principles was made by Le Corbusier in his famous "Five Points for a New Architecture" from 1926.[5] Its aim was the reinterpretation of the original relation of a building to the earth, the sky, and the horizon. Thus, Le Corbusier's pillars (*pilotis*) and roof gardens (*toits-jardins*) entail the relation of the building to below and above, while his strip window (*fenêtre en longeur*) places it within the limiting horizon. Finally, the free plan (*plan libre*) expresses an open world, where functions can be freely accommodated.[6]

Recast in our terminology, this means that the organization of space is no longer the province of distinct elements and symmetries but becomes a floating assembly of functional zones; this is what lies at the heart of the slogan that "buildings should be designed from the inside out." At the same time, the building becomes free from its traditional static contact with the ground and is seen as a system of points and lines of force. This system is a precondition of the free plan. Its final result is the dissolution of the gestalt,

G. Asplund, Stockholm Exhibition 1930

or, in other words, that conventional types are eliminated.[7] True enough, the desire for a comprehensible whole is still present, though this wholeness is understood in purely geometrical terms. For Le Corbusier, geometry and construction represent the classic, while the free plan and facade represent instead something Nordic. In this respect, his architecture was truly "international."[8]

That form should follow function should not be understood too literally. The modernists did not intend that form should be discovered anew for each task, but rather that general principles would insure proper accommodation of function, and that these principles constituted an "aesthetic." Thus Le Corbusier wrote: "The five points involve an entirely new aesthetic. Nothing of the architecture of earlier epochs remains."[9] It is evident that the forms of expression mentioned above were the result of a general aim, one that sought to bring architecture into accordance with the new age. As a result, many Nordic architects accepted modernism as a liberating resolution of the conflict between the national and the foreign.

The idea of functional modernism was introduced to the North in 1925. In the Norwegian periodical *Byggekunst,* Lars Backer wrote about "Our Vacillating Architecture," polemically arguing for the new objective direction: "We want to create an architecture in contact with the time we live in,

L. Backer, Skansen Resturant, Oslo

G. Blakstad and H. Munthe-Kaas, House of Artists, Oslo

G. Blakstad and H. Munthe-Kaas, Odd Fellow
Building, Oslo

natural for the material we build in. We want to escape the masks and the applied; expedience should define form. Plan and facade should be one."[10] The same year, Edvard Heiberg reported from the Paris Exhibition, praising Le Corbusier's Pavillon de l'Esprit Nouveau for its "refreshing naturalness." Gregor Paulsson underlined the importance of the pavilion in the Danish journal *Architekten,* and in Sweden Uno Åhrén wrote: "It is as if the functional attains aesthetic value. . . . The forms, which are defined by their purpose, are already complete, requiring no further beautification."[11] In the years that followed, Åhrén and Heiberg continued to promote the new architecture, and in 1927, Backer completed Scandinavia's first modern building, the Skansen Restaurant in Oslo.

F. Reppen, housing blocks, Professor Dahls gate, Oslo

The manifesto of nordic functionalism is the book *acceptera,* written in conjunction with the great Stockholm Exhibition in 1930, where the life-style of the time was presented in architecture and utilitarian objects.[12] The exhibition's main architect was Gunnar Asplund, though many other Swedish pioneer modernists participated. The reverberations of this exhibition were felt far outside of Sweden, and the exhibition still remains one of the most important manifestations of the new objectivity. As a result, its fiftieth anniversary was commemorated with a publication entitled *Nordisk Funktionalism.* Gunilla Lundahl writes in its foreword: "Characteristic of the Nordic interpretation of functionalism was its sober scale, its sense for nature and humanism."[13] This statement is intriguing in that it suggests that Nordic modernism retained regional particulars, and that they also comprised a conscious social program. Thus its aim was to give the new aesthetic a solid foundation.

Functionalism's background and aims found their manifestation in *acceptera.* The authors, Gunnar Asplund, Wolter Gahn, Sven Markelius, Gregor Paulsson, Eskil Sundahl, and Uno Åhrén, give an ostensibly complete account of the new time and its forms of expression. In chapters on society, housing, industrialization and standardization, form, the relation of the new and old, and the city, these problems are discussed in depth, and many examples are included. The book ends with the manifesto entitled "acceptera," which reads: "accept the existing reality—only by so doing can we begin to master it, to control it in such a way that we can change it, and create a culture that is a flexible tool for life. We have no need of the old culture's outgrown forms in order to maintain our self-respect."[14] In the text, Asplund criticizes his own democratic City Library (Stadsbiblioteket), because it "has the outer form of an antique castle."

E. Moestue and O. Lind Schistad, Ingierstrand Baths, Oslo

Functionalism, then, went radically to work, to be rid of any kind of heritage, as regards forms of life, architecture, and art. But what happened to sobriety and feeling for nature? The answer is simple: the first modernists grew up with classicism and national romanticism, and whether they wanted it or not, this heritage came through in their works. (The same can be said of the European pioneers as well.) Therefore, it was hardly the desire for imitation of the past that defined the appearance of Asplund's library but rather his formal schooling. The succeeding generation, however, had no corresponding foundation. The result was the "crisis of functionalism."[15] Thus wrote George Eliassen:

> It would appear, however, that the burden placed upon the shoulders of architects in this time of transition was, in most cases, too heavy to be borne. Without the support of a firm codex of style, it was only the exceptions who managed to complete their projects along independent lines, in an architecturally justifiable form. Here, as elsewhere, we sank into an epoch of epigones. . . . Functionalism, style—architecture's bad conscience, became itself a victim of formalism. It became not only style, but fashion."[16]

Despite the decay Eliassen describes, certain Nordic values managed to survive the tabula rasa of the thirties, namely, the sense of dwelling and the desire for contact with nature. Both were brought forth under the light of national romanticism, and for that reason, it is not unjustified to call interwar Nordic architecture romantic modernism. This characterization applies to the Swede Gunnar Asplund, the Finn Alvar Aalto, the Dane Kay Fisker, and the Norwegian Ove Bang, to name but a few of the most important architects. It was this romantic undercurrent that laid the basis for postwar regionalism, and which represents the North's greatest contribution to contemporary architecture. For the first time since the Gothic, the Nordic thus attained international significance.

Before we account for the Nordic contribution, it is necessary to clarify the difference between international modernism's social goals and the humanism of the North. Le Corbusier defined the aim of his basic principles as a recovery of "elemental joys: sun, air, and greenery"; joys lost in the nineteenth-century's industrial city. Le Corbusier had unquestionably essential values in mind, but his followers recast these elemental joys in purely quantitative terms; indeed, functionalism's crisis is due to, among other things, this process of oversimplification.[17] The romantic modernism of the North, conversely, was less rational and conserved the qualitative relation that elsewhere was forgotten. Let us, for the moment, stress that the qualitative is always concrete, in the sense of "contact with the immediately given," and is thus necessarily linked to a sense for nature.

Lars Backer was the first to build a relatively large functionalist building in Scandinavia. We have already mentioned his Skansen Restaurant (built 1925–27; demolished 1971). Here, the new architecture was introduced in the clearest possible way: the free plan, an ordering structure, and modernism's characteristic forms such as geometric volumes, flat roof, and continuous strip windows are all present. Above a ground floor containing entry and cloakroom, and a mezzanine with the kitchen, the restaurant was designed as a large, open room. A system of slender freestanding columns gave the interior order and rhythm while freeing the walls structurally. "The space is without details; it is view, people, color and the lamps by the Danish designer Poul Henningsen which make the room," wrote Backer. A series of terraces connected Skansen to the surrounding terrain; both here and in the openness of the main space contact with nature is manifest. Upon completion of Skansen, Backer began work on the Ekeberg Restaurant, which still stands, though it has been somewhat rebuilt. Again the clear concrete skeleton is evident, as well as large, open floor spaces and continuous areas of glass; and again, the relationship to the terrain is of essential significance. Backer's promising career came unfortunately to an abrupt halt: he died in 1930, and Norwegian modernism suffered a painful loss.[18]

In 1928, Norwegian architects organized a study trip to Holland, where they surveyed the buildings of Berlage, Oud, Duiker, and Dudok, among others. The result of the excursion was a near total conversion to modernism. A series of competition projects from the following years bear witness to this, and soon many important buildings were built. Of special interest is the Artists House (Kunstneres Hus) in Oslo by Blakstad and Munthe-Kaas (1929–1930). The architects' classical background resonates in its symmetrical disposition, but the result is otherwise modernist. The ground floor, with vestibule and restaurant, is thus formed within a regular concrete skeleton filled in with glass panels. A cantilevered canopy extends from this skeleton, exhibiting new structural possibilities; these were indeed a precondition for the large top-lit exhibition halls, which are sheathed in brick. A refined ornamental treatment of the brick surfaces expresses their nonbearing character. In 1931, Blakstad and Munthe-Kaas won the competition for the Odd Fellow Building in Oslo and thereupon became Norway's leading functionalists. The building, finished in 1934, illustrates well the principles of modern architecture: a recessed, load-bearing skeleton, free plans, and continuous strip windows. The clear, well-proportioned building fits well into the surroundings and proves that the modern vocabulary can be both rich and elegant.[19]

Another significant group of modernists came to the fore in Norway about 1930. Among these were Eyvind Moestue and Ole Lind, whose charming recreational facility Ingierstrand (1933) reinterpreted the Norwegian sense for nature, while at the same time its diving tower displays a

A. Korsmo, Villa Dammann, Oslo

A. Korsmo, Villa Dammann, Oslo

O. Bang, Worker's Association, Oslo

A. Korsmo, Villa Stenersen, Oslo

traditional Norwegian sense for structural form. Ingierstrand belongs to a series of complexes in which architecture and the natural environment interplay; another is the original Dronningen Restaurant (1929–32), by Andr. H. Bjerke and George Eliassen. It is situated out on the water, in connection with Oslo's light craft harbor, uniting the modern with a romantic sense for mood and the effects of light. The relationship to natural surroundings also plays a role in housing projects as well, as for example in Frithjof Reppen's housing blocks in Professor Dahls Gate in Oslo (1929–32), a fine study in the accommodation of terrain, together with a sensitive articulation of the built form.

Ove Bang has come to be regarded as the strongest personality among Norwegian architects of the thirties.[20] Bang was an enthusiastic outdoorsman, developing during his first working years in Rjukan a deep understanding for his homeland's nature and landscape. When he opened his architectural practice in Oslo in 1930, he immediately gave the new vocabulary a Norwegian tone. Thus he offered promising answers to the issue of dwelling, in a series of cabins and villas. In a cabin at Geilo, for example, large glass surfaces are incorporated in a log wall. A traditional Norwegian gallery is the element that allows for the juxtaposition of the new and the old. Bang's domestic work culminated with the large Villa Ditlev-Simonsen (1937), where a free spatial composition is accommodated within a gestalt that despite its modern tones awakens Norwegian associations. The same qualities emerge at a larger scale in Bang's major work, the Worker's Association (Samfunnshuset) in Oslo (1939). Here, structural clarity and formal freedom are conjoined in a building that, thanks to its gestalt quality, measures up to the best of its time, even in an international context.

It is fitting to conclude our references to interwar Norwegian architecture with some remarks about Arne Korsmo, one of the pioneers who established links to the postwar period.[21] Korsmo appeared at the end of the twenties with several dwellings of high quality. Among these, the Villa Dammann (1930) is in a class of its own. Hardly any other modern building in Norway exhibits such striking originality. Influences from Mendelsohn and Dudok are indeed visible, but above all, it is Korsmo's remarkable sense for articulate form and poetic space that emerges. The large living room is almost totally closed to the south, while the end walls to the east and west are opened with vertical glazed slots from floor to ceiling "in order to experience the surroundings from hill to hill." The view to the south is instead offered by a small semicircular room whose strip window provides a 180-degree panorama. This space is small but open, whereas the living room is closed but grand. A fascinating tension between characters is thereby achieved, suggesting that Korsmo had a particularly fine sense of place. Apart from Villa Dammann, Villa Stenersen is Korsmo's main achievement. Here, a convincing synthesis of clear construction, generous form, free plan, and free facade is realized, while the utilization of the terrain is well handled. Korsmo's career culminated in 1938 with the We Can (Vikan) exhibition in Oslo, where he received free rein for his abilities, elucidating the environment in harmony with the new precepts.[22] We Can, however, terminated an epoch; the belief in a new age came to an abrupt halt as the modern world succumbed to the Armageddon of World War II.

Swedish modernism began with the preparations for the Stockholm Exhibition, with art historian Gregor Paulsson acting as the ideologue and Gunnar Asplund as the architect. During the three years before 1930, much occurred that influenced the plans, most important was the appearance of Sven Markelius. After a trip to Europe in 1927, when he visited the Weisshoffsiedlung in Stuttgart and the Bauhaus in Dessau, Markelius reworked his winning project for the Helsingborg Concert Hall (1926) in such a way that upon dedication in 1932, it became Sweden's first public building in the functionalist style.[23] The project consists of two units: the closed volume of the concert hall proper and, perpendicular to it, the more complex wing containing a vestibule and foyer. The building is a true example of "form follows function," at least with respect to spatial organization: visitors are led from the central entrance to the symmetrically flanking cloakrooms at either side, then once again into the foyer. The solution is both functional and self-evident, and results in a fine spatial effect that can bear comparison with the representative entry halls of the baroque era. The concert hall proper is fully clad in mahogany, ensuring both good acoustics and a warmth that befits its application. In general, the Helsingborg Concert Hall represents an important contribution to the development of modern monumental architecture and shows that a functional solution can be united with a comprehensible gestalt.

While Markelius was at work on the Concert Hall, he made several other progressive projects. In 1928, he won, in collaboration with Uno Åhrén, the competition for the Residence Hall at The Technical College (Tekniska Högskolans Kårhus) in Stockholm; construction was finished in 1930.

S. Markelius, Concert Hall, Helsingborg, Sweden

S. Markelius, Concert Hall, Helsingborg, Sweden

Here, movement through space is an important factor: stairs are placed on the exterior, giving entry to the various levels. The closed exterior, the strip windows on the short faces, and the dining hall's large glazed openings onto the internal court are good examples of functionally conditioned differentiation. Markelius's own house in Nockeby (1930) is another essay in practical planning, but at the same time, the space seems "homey and sunny" in a Nordic way.[24] Among the architect's other work in the thirties, we should mention the Collective Building (Kollektivhuset) in Stockholm (1936). A new concept of apartment housing was proposed here, in which women could be freed from housework, and many of the radical cultural personalities of the time exploited the solution.

Markelius was unquestionably the most versatile personality of Swedish functionalism, but he was not the first. Already in 1925 to 1928, Osvald Almqvist had built two power stations in the modern style and moreover participated in the 1930 Stockholm Exhibition with a row house.[25] A more intriguing project, however, was the Element House of Erik Friberger (Göteborg 1937). Its bearing steel skeleton and prefabricated wall panels represent an original achievement, and it therefore was included in Alfred Roth's pioneering book on the new architecture.[26]

Among the architects who contributed to the development of Swedish modernism, Gunnar Asplund is considered the most distinct and significant figure. This is not because he was the most modern, but rather because he expanded and enriched the aims of functionalism. In short, the enrichment consisted in the introduction of another dimension of meaning in modern architecture. This fact is not surprising, considering that he had already exhibited a remarkable sense for expression and content in his early works, especially through the sensitive use of "memories." It may seem that

G. Asplund, extension to the Court House,
Göteborg

his buildings for the Stockholm Exhibition represented a break with this attitude, but behind the radical statements in *acceptera* (for which Asplund was not solely responsible) a poetic tone resonates; thus, his Danish colleague Aage Rafn characterized the exhibition as a "functionalist dream." And indeed it was a dream; its light transparent structures gave modern freedom a deeper meaning: "Slip into dusk, the deep blue night sky, and the thousand nuances of light will come to those that dance, or sip their drinks. People want not to lose their contact with nature, especially in summer." [27]

With the expansion of the Göteborg Court House (Göteborgs Rådhus), Asplund succeeded in uniting an uncompromising contemporary approach with a meaningful relation to the existing building. The project thus represents an important step toward a more nuanced modern architecture; with justification, it is considered an early example of creative adaptation. The means employed are not only a continuation of the dimensions, rhythms, and proportions of the old Court House but a rethinking of it as built form; as a result, Asplund shows that behind any style there exists certain objective formal and spatial essences that would be understood and interpreted. The interior expresses this in its terms: thus it unites timeless monumentality with a contemporary democratic character. In addition, the warm wooden cladding and sensitive detailing endow the space with a typically Nordic mood.

The Woodland Cemetery (Skogskyrkogården) in Stockholm (1935–40) is Asplund's major work and one of the most significant manifestations of Nordic architecture. The comprehensive complex dates from a competition that Asplund won in 1915, in collaboration with Sigurd Lewerentz. While the latter deserves much of the credit for the treatment of the landscape, the Woodland Chapel (1918–20) and the Woodland Crematorium (completed 1935) are Asplund's work.[28] The complicated origins of the layout do not hinder the sense of wholeness; indeed, nature and architecture mesh in a manner unparalleled in our time, revealing essential features of each. Both are moreover linked to the life of human souls, so that the totality becomes complete. The quality of the Woodland Cemetery is especially evident if one compares it with older works in which landscape and building symbiotically clarify each other, such as Renaissance and baroque villa projects. Whereas these are formed as unambiguous developments along one or more axes, with the building forming a point of origin and goal, in relation to a more or less tamed nature, the Woodland Cemetery is more modern in its free distribution of elements. This is already evident in the main movement from the entrance toward a centrally placed cross. The concave semicircle of the entry is a traditional motif, but instead of allowing passage to proceed axially therefrom, the footpath ahead diverges, so that the depression in the landscape dominates, whereby the human-made is gathered around timeless nature, which itself becomes present as earth and sky. The crematorium attains its meaning in relation to the meditation mound that concentrates the whole within a simple gestalt. The walls along the footpaths link and lead, and the antehall of the main chapel captures the movement without halting it. It is a clear, pillared structure, simultaneously abstract grove and primary architectonic form, while its skylight "explains" both meanings. The floor pattern in the chapel engages in the anteroom's articulate masonry, leading us into the space that forms the epicenter of the complex. Here, the enclosive apse gathers the movement of the surroundings, while the capitals and entasis of the attendant columns echo classical corporality. All achieves nearness, while referring beyond itself. Meaning is focused in Sven Erixson's fresco of the ship of the dead, disappearing into a tunnel of light; perhaps it is an echo of Väinämöinen's death. Thus, departure, reminiscence, and hope combine and at the same time internalize the surrounding landscape. As a result, stands of birch and pine, lawns, rises, reflecting ponds, and paths emerge as what they are and inform us that it is our task to understand and "say" things.[29]

G. Asplund, Woodland Cemetery, Stockholm

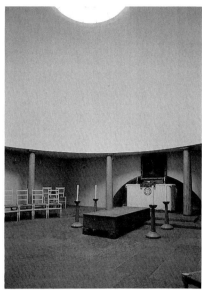

G. Asplund, Woodland Chapel, Stockholm

The small Woodland Chapel seems a concentrated sketch for the entire complex, which was completed later. Here, the traditional enclosure expresses that we have arrived at a different place, while the chapel's anteroom signifies the continuation of the forest around. The shingled hiproof suggests that its goal is the Nordic cave of wood. Inside, however, it is transformed into a light-filled cupola space, surrounded by stylized Doric columns. The Woodland Chapel thus conceals classical form within the local, and the building's "explanation" consists in this mixture. Seldom has architectural meaning been evoked with such poetic concentration.

As a whole the Woodland Cemetery illustrates the relation of the Nordic to the universal, and in a Swedish manner, that is, as an eclectic assemblage. Nevertheless, the "memories" here become essential. The small chapel is still romantic-classical, while the crematorium has become modern in its free spatial organization. Thus the recovery of the origins is realized.

Alvar Aalto's work from the thirties seems equally essential and equally concrete. But his work takes on a Finnish tone; indeed, it does so in such an evident manner that his works were signaled as the beginning of a new phase in the "new tradition."[30] Aalto was converted to modernism after hearing, in 1928, a lecture by Sven Markelius at the Finnish Architectural Society's annual meeting in Turku (Åbo). Aalto and Markelius had already been in contact for a few years, but thanks to his travels in 1927, the Swede was better oriented about events underway in Europe. The lecture in Turku was entitled "The Search for the Rational in Modern Architecture" and presented, in the main, the ideas of Gropius. The talk was evidently liberating for its listeners; in 1928, Aalto reworked his classical winning project for the library in Viipuri (Viborg) in the modern style (built 1934–35).[31] The library has been considered the first manifestation of regional modernism. This is not so much a result of the exterior as it is of the handling of interior space, where a modernist continuum receives a domestic tone through the introduction of light and the use of natural materials. Especially characteristic is the lecture hall's undulate wooden ceiling, which not only provides a warm mood but represents essential Finnish environmental qualities as well.

By the time Aalto had built the Viipuri library, he had already realized a much larger complex: the sanatorium in Paimio (Pemar) (1929–32). Here, he shows himself as a modernist par excellence. All facades are defined from within: the endless strip windows of the corridors, the separate windows of the patients' rooms, the stacked verandas of the wards, and the service wing's erratically placed openings. No overall order is present; the whole seems a heterogeneous conjunction of functionally defined volumes, outwardly expressive. In this free functionality lies the key to Aalto's work: he allows content and movement to define the solution, while its openness reflects the land's own structure. No other pioneers of modernism has done anything of the like; for all the others, traditional formal restraints were somehow involved.

Aalto's intentions found their most beautiful and complete expression in Villa Mairea in Noormarkku (1938–39). The house is large and compound, but nevertheless unitary. Again, each zone has its own character: the hearthroom opens onto an internal court, the living room brings the forest within, the dining room groups around the table, the conservatory allows summer to survive winter, the books of the library engage us—all is articulate as a continuous, but differentiated, space marked by warmth and domesticity. In general, the house can be understood as a three-dimensional collage, and as such it furthers the Wrightian "destruction of the box." But while Frank Lloyd Wright and his European followers formed the house as an abstract compound of horizontal and vertical planes, Aalto dissolves space into qualitative places wherein life can take place naturally. These places are empathetic with the surroundings, both in rhythm and use of materials: thus the pine trunks echo in the interior's freely disposed columns and stair supports. On the exterior, the entrance facade's modernistic motifs relax into the domestic forms of the courtyard wing and sauna. In this way, the house turns back to its roots, extending itself into the forest.

Aalto's architecture in the thirties culminated with the Finnish Pavilion for the World Exhibition in New York, 1939. Here, his organic formal vocabulary includes ideas outside of the conceptual world of Le Corbusier's "Five Points," but which are nonetheless modern, and here the ground was laid for the "new regionalism."

Aalto's contributions overshadow all other Finnish modernists, but this is not to say that he was the only one to do quality work. We can here

A. Aalto, Sanatorium, Paimio, Finland

A. Aalto, Villa Mairea, Noormarku, Finland

A. Aalto, Villa Mairea, Noormarku, Finland

A. Aalto, Villa Mairea, Noormarku, Finland

A. Aalto, Sanatorium, Paimio, Finland

only mention the distinguished Turku architect Erik Bryggman, who realized the thoroughly functionalist Finnish Sports Institute (Suomen urheiluopisto) in Vierumäki (1933–36), and whose Turku Academy Book Tower (1936) showed that a building designed from the inside out can also achieve true gestalt quality. Especially well known is his Chapel of the Resurrection in Turku (1939–41), where basic Christian forms are reinterpreted in a sensitive and convincing manner.

It is hardly a surprise that Danish functionalism's contribution to interwar architecture was less remarkable than that of the other Nordic lands. The Danish tradition of building has always been characterized by sobriety and respect for domestic forms, and has thus reflected only minor influence from the shifting stylistic currents. Danish architecture, however, had possessed a latent modernism in the form of clear, repetitive structures and ascetic detailing. Hence, the transition from late classicism to functionalism was almost unnoticeable, so that closer inspection of Danish contemporary architecture is necessary to reveal its significance. It is also a part of the Danish character that buildings that serve daily life receive more attention than they might in other countries, while monumental buildings are correspondingly modest. The emergence of the modern vocabulary is therefore especially evident in housing, where late classicism's endless window repetition gave way to the systematic use of balconies (cf. the development from Kay Fisker's Hornbaekhus (1923) to his Vestersøhus in Copenhagen (1935, in collaboration with C. F. Møller.))[32] In general, we may say that Danish facades from the thirties tend to an enhanced contact between inside and out, though without impairing their Danish character.

A few architects were, however, working more radically, for example, Mogens Lassen built several fine houses where Le Corbusier's influence is evident, and his System House (1937) employs a concrete skeleton infilled with glass panels, the whole being worked out with Danish consistency. Vilhelm Lauritzen, an affirmed modernist, gave Denmark its first large functionalist building with his Copenhagen Airport Terminal Building at Kastrup (1936–39); as mentioned in the first chapter, Lauritzen here achieved the linkage of the new with a remarkable sense of domesticity.

Arne Jacobsen is generally considered Danish modernism's most distinguished representative.[33] In 1929, in cooperation with Flemming Lassen, he won the competition for the "house of the future": a circular, rotatable building with space for an airplane on the roof. In 1934, he realized the beautiful purist Bellavista complex in Klampenborg, which appears as a softened version of German housing projects from the twenties. Already in the beginning of the thirties, Jacobsen's housing expressed the desire for humanization of the international style, and his earlier pure abstract forms were replaced by the domestic pitched roof and by brick as a main building material. This tendency culminated with the Århus City Hall (competition project 1937, in collaboration with Erik Møller, built 1939–42). Here, repetitive Danish order reemerges, and the skeletal cladding of the tower echoes traditional Danish half-timbering.

A. Jacobsen, City Hall, Århus, Denmark

But the Danish contribution to Nordic modernism consisted only of a refined humanization of the new vocabulary. Through the thirties, an empathy with nature resonates. This is of course the basis of the Danish building tradition, but over and above the direct presence this entails, Danish architects also aimed at a linkage of building to place. At Århus University, this becomes incomparably manifest. In 1931, Kay Fisker, Poul Stegman, and Christian Frederik Møller, in collaboration with the landscape architect Carl Theodor Sørensen, won the competition for the extensive institution, and though building continued over a long period, the project represents an early example of true regionalism.[34] The university was long considered by many modernists as a betrayal of the principles of the new architecture, but today we can value it as a convincing synthesis of new and

C. F. Møller et al., University, Århus, Denmark

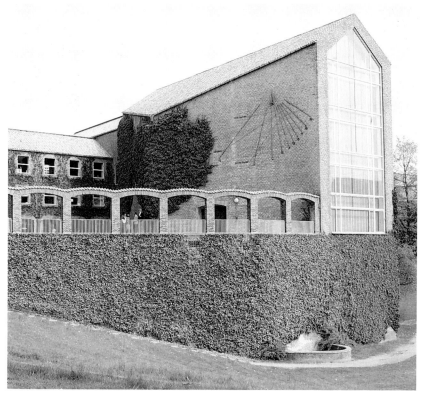

domestic traditions. The simple, elemental buildings are indisputably Danish, while their accommodation to the terrain entails that the asthetic of the free plan is transposed upon exterior space. If the complex does not exhibit the same local differentiation as Asplund and Lewerentz's Woodland Cemetery, it is the result of the differing programmatic contents. But Århus University does share with the cemetery the achievement of interplay and wholeness, and thereby the representation of the genius of the local environment.

Functionalism had two aims: to recover the most primitive things, and to create a new dwelling. We have seen that the recovery was partially successful, insofar as it introduced basic principles that replaced the styles of the past. But we have also seen that as a result of their international character, these principles were unable to secure the linkage with place that is necessary in order that inhabitants may *dwell.* Here we confront the question of whether functionalism really could manage to satisfy the need for a new dwelling. Implicit in the foregoing is the idea that to dwell entails something more than a roof over one's head and elemental joys, and it was precisely in confrontation with this "something more" that functionalism fell short, though this is not to dismiss work on new housing as unsuccessful.

Interwar modern architecture contributed in many ways to the resolution of urgent social problems, and housing was always of central interest. The Weissenhofsiedlung housing project in Stuttgart (1927) was thus entitled Die Neue Wohnung. Here, and in other German housing projects from the same time, a more practical and healthful type of dwelling was developed than the blocks and endless rowhouses of the industrial city, and the first CIAM congress (Congrés International pour l'Architecture Moderne) was essential in leading housing in a more humane direction.[35] These new ideas came to play a greater role in the Nordic countries than elsewhere, and in the course of the thirties a series of prototypical projects was realized. We have already mentioned Norwegian and Danish examples and could add many more. Aalto's contributions deserve special attention, both because his solutions were new and because he took the accommodation of place more seriously than did most others. The workers' housing at the Cellulose Factory in Sunila (1937–39) offers a good example.

But it was in Sweden that the construction of new housing was most comprehensive, and the result was a new urban structure, based on Le Corbusier's concept of a "green city." But whereas the Swiss-French master worked with huge *unités,* or "vertical villages," Swedish housing is for the most part of three or four stories. The intention was already formulated in *acceptera:* "The demand for access to direct sunlight for all dwellings will make its marks upon new housing. It has compelled an open manner of building, with parallel lengths of buildings, positioned with respect to the sun."[36] Ostensibly, this solution is in accordance with the Nordic desire for nearness

Göta Square, Göteborg

F. Berner, Torvalmenningen, Bergen

with nature, but in practice it became clear that these new housing areas had neither the qualities of the city nor the country. Instead, they were some hybrid, without any identity of place. What was lost was urban space. Recognition of this fact is essential because it informs us that contact with nature does not consist in spreading buildings throughout the landscape but in building in a manner that makes visible the understood landscape. It is unfortunate that the loss of place occurred when the recovery of true urbanism began, such as with the Götaplatsen in Göteborg (Sigfrid Ericson, Ernst Torulf, Arvid Bjerke 1917–23, with the City Theater by Carl Bergsten

S. Markelius et al., Hötorget, Stockholm

C. Bergsten, City Theater, Göteborg

1935) and the Torvalmenningen in Bergen (Finn Berner 1922–29, with Sundt's department store by Per Grieg 1938). This development ended with the first postwar open city plans, such as the high-rise housing at the Hötorget in Stockholm (Sven Markelius and David Hellén, after 1946).[37]

    The crisis of functionalism, then, was less a consequence of its measurable results than of its inability to satisfy needs that go beyond the elementary joys. Our account of Nordic architecture's identity and history has shown that its aim has always been the creation of an architecture that brings the inhabited landscape close to human society, through the use of forms that represent and complement the given environment. In order that this can occur, architecture must have local roots. Certainly, some basic principles are international, but they must adapt to the situation. In our time, the free plan is a basic principle because it represents the new global and dynamic world, but it must be interpreted in accordance with the genius of place. Giedion recognized this already in 1954, when he raised the claim for a "new regionalism," and in that connection brought forth the work of Aalto.[38] Our presentation of the romantic modernism of the North shows that Aalto was not alone. In each of the Nordic lands, there was an undercurrent in the thirties that sought to unite the international with the domestic, not by superficial combination but through the expression of the essence of the environment. And any environment is both regional and universal. Nordic modernism made thus an essential contribution to the development of the new tradition.

A. Aalto, House of Culture, Helsinki

In the decades following the Second World War, our architectural milieu has been subject to radical changes. The traditional buildings, which previously punctuated the landscape, have disappeared; only a few examples of domestic folk architecture remain, and the church has been pushed aside in favor of centers that cater to movement and passage rather than acting as a common goal. Recognizable typological form has been replaced by random invention; indeed, even the international style has disappeared, or at least its program for deliberate wholeness. Today modernism has been reduced to a collection of dismembered motifs. Of course, this decay is not as pronounced in all the Nordic lands; it is most conspicuous in Norway and least evident in Denmark, where the traditional sense for disciplined order has been maintained. But irrespective of location, the present is characterized by insecurity and confusion. The general condition may be called a loss of place. A locality is no longer a meeting place and a home but is instead reduced to a set of "offerings," while its *genius,* which had made possible human identification and belonging, is a thing of the past.

The causes of this situation are numerous. When it became clear that an environment in accordance with our time could not be achieved by means of the international style, architects were left, so to speak, empty handed. As the Norwegian architect and critic George Eliassen has pointed out, only an elite few managed to create a justifiable architecture without the support of a codex of style, that is to say, a tradition of building, resulting in architecture's weakened position with respect to society. In addition to these professional causes, there is of course the general insecurity of our age in which immediate stimulation and consumption are more relevant than continuity and meaning. Today, however, we are finally recognizing that fragmentary understanding can endanger our very existence. It is therefore important to discuss the role of architecture as such, and ask: Is it possible to create an environment that is both contemporary and rooted?

The regional undercurrent of the thirties showed that a modern architecture with roots in the place is possible. What began as the international style could thereby achieve true closeness to life and become a tradition, for true tradition consists in something more than the repetition of types. Its characters must engage in time and place, and thereby unite permanence and change. The particular significance of the Nordic contribution is the emergence of the new regionalism at a time when the modern movement had been arrested in Germany, Italy, and the Soviet Union as a result of political pressure, at a time when the American pioneers had been forgotten in favor of a more or less superficial eclecticism.[1] Therefore, Aalto's pavilion at the 1939 New York World's Fair stood as a lonely representative for our time.

The idea of a new tradition is based on the conviction that our time has identity, despite all political unrest and cultural confusion. When we attempt to suggest its character with words like "global," "open," "dynamic,"

8

The Regional

and "unfinished," it is because we mean that our time differs from the more stable civilizations of the past. Today, we can no longer agree upon definite dogmas or values but must remain open to dissimilarity and multiplicity. As a result, our condition has been called pluralistic.[2] But does this suggest that all form of tradition has become impossible? Hardly. First, the understanding that constitutes our being-in-the-world is always there; second, given place still retains its identity. Today, too, life takes place, and we must understand all difference and change in relation to the primary structures of this occurrence. We have called these structures *origins,* and indeed, it was in searching for an "original" common denominator that modernism sought to recover the most primitive things.

Giedion recognized that recovery needed to occur in several phases. The first consisted in the definition of general principles, the second in enrooting these locally, and the third in developing a "new monumentality."[3] To avoid misunderstanding, it should be underscored that "monumental" here denotes "meaningful," and that meaning in architecture presupposes that the inhabited landscape is brought close to human society; regionalism and monumentality are therefore complementary. In the first chapter we investigated what this entails, and in chapter 7 we suggested how it may occur in our time. The Woodland Crematorium serves as a clarifying example.

It follows from our presentation that the Nordic world possesses an essential affinity with our time, if not the modern world. Both are characterized by incompleteness and dynamism, whereas the high cultures of the South have always had a more static character. This is why the traditional longing for the South has been supplanted by an increased interest in the North, where the modern is indeed present in an original manner, so that those who live in a time of dissolution can learn that openness and dynamism can be combined with identity of place and sense of home.

In the following we shall look at the postwar Nordic contributions to the development of a new regionalism and related manifestations of a new monumentality. Some Nordic architects, empowered by their sense of the quality of place, have also been in a position to interpret foreign worlds. Jørn Utzon's Sydney Opera House (1957–66) is an early example, and he and Reima Pietilä have both built important buildings that give the Islamic world an authentic contemporary interpretation. This also holds true for Henning Larsen's State Department in Riyad, Saudi Arabia (1980–84), an especially important contribution to regional monumentality.[4] These works give our presentation a more complete perspective; for in fact, Nordic and Islamic architecture have certain basal features in common. More precisely, both are anticlassical, in that they undermine classical corporality through the use of line and web. But whereas the Islamic web is light and emerges as a net of straight lines, the Nordic is dark and shows itself as a topological pattern where hidden forces seem to be at work. We might also say that the Islamic web renders that which remains after light has consumed all concrete forms, whereas the Nordic expresses the possibilities of incompleteness.[5] Between these two extremes, we find the classical world, where light casts for each thing its own shadow and thereby allows it to emerge as a distinct gestalt. Accordingly, we can complete our mythic geography with an image of three environments: the darkness of the North, the shadow of the South, and the light of the desert. In this image, the South occupies the middle, representing the belief that that which is can show itself. For that reason, southerners assume that classical embodiment represents the original as such, a belief that results in a dogmatic understanding of reality. In our time, however, all forms of dogmatism are impossible, and Nordic freedom attains relevance. In this connection, let us remember Goethe's prophetic words: "It is not always necessary that truth be embodied; it is sufficient that it hover about nearby, like a spirit bringing forth accord, as when bells toll with friendly solemnity through the air."[6]

But despite the understanding that emerges with the leading Nordic architects, the situation, as noted, is anything but clear. So far, pluralism has consisted of a rapid alternation of isms, if not fashions, while leading theoreticians have proclaimed the "death of architecture."[7] It is not our task to account here for brutalism, structuralism, postmodernism, and deconstructivism. Let us simply note that the first three aimed to supplement the insufficiencies of functionalism by a new expressivity and distinct figural quality. Especially interesting were Robert Venturi's attempts to create an architecture that was both new and old, through the use of conventional forms in new contexts.[8] None of these isms, however, managed to develop solidly, and in the eighties architecture degenerated into an uninhibited application of borrowed motifs. It is therefore not surprising that a reaction came in the form of deconstruction, whose creed is that architecture should not mean anything at all.[9]

Is the conclusion, then, that, despite all promising undercurrents, architecture is dead? If we consider the chaos that characterizes our current surroundings, it may seem futile to call out for a new regionalism and a new monumentality. But hope still exists that it is possible to recover an understanding of *origins*. Louis Kahn developed precisely this understanding; his writings imply a theory that might serve as a guide for the future. We have elsewhere attempted to deepen and systematize Kahn's ideas with the help of Heidegger's thoughts concerning dwelling and building.[10] And as we have already suggested, Nordic architecture is of relevance because it has made regionalism a living reality.

Postwar isms were more than anything a reaction to the schematism of official modern architecture, in which simplified versions of the basic principles were passed off as the work itself. In the North, examples of this degenerate late modernism are innumerable; we can mention the housing development Albertslund outside Copenhagen (1963–68), where the spatial

Albertslund, Copenhagen

organization makes human orientation difficult and the built-form identification impossible, at the same time that any gestalt quality has been lost. While this schematism is latent in the Danish tradition, the Swedish has a pitfall of its own: the reduction of buildings to banal volumes and the loss of all the memories that might enrich the form. In Finland, too, a new rigidity came about in the fifties and sixties, when the classical component of tradition took the upper hand. In Norway, confusion resulted when the domestic building tradition was lost. This propensity for confusion is also a result of a lack of an urban tradition. This becomes evident in the Oslo City Hall (Oslo Radhus) (Arnstein Arneberg and Magnus Poulsson 1915–50).[11] The City Hall has a certain gestalt quality and has in time become one of the city's landmarks; the semicircular square facing the city also functions well. But the whole is nevertheless a heterogeneous juxtaposition of features that reflect its long process of becoming: national romanticism, late classicism, and functionalism, coupled with an anachronistic artistic decoration, are conjoined without internal correspondence. (That a juxtaposition of differing components can form a meaningful whole is illustrated by Carl Bergsten's fine City Theater (Stadsteater) in Göteborg (1935), where a series of Ionic columns are asymetrically placed within the upper story's modernistic windows: truly a predecessor of Venturi's difficult "both/and" architecture).

Schematism and confusion are indexes that express the general situation and imply that spatial organization and/or built form have lost their gestalt quality.[12] It is this decline that regional modernism has as its task to conquer, through the realization of the second and third phases of the new tradition.

We have already seen that Alvar Aalto was the only architect who managed to take the leap from Le Corbusier's "Five Points" to a more organic conception of space and form. Thus, he endowed the free plan with new content, interpreting it topologically rather than geometrically. As a result, his spatial organizations seem like living organisms, where functions are not merely served but are also represented and complemented. And he allowed built form to attend the spatial composition, such that a collage of qualitatively different, but complementary, places are formed. Finally, he sought to recover gestalt quality in memorable figures such as the town hall in Säynätsalo (1950), where a relatively free assemblage of wings, adapted to the place, are gathered by the vertical volume of the council hall. The House of Culture (Kulttuuritalo) in Helsinki (1955) also consists of qualitatively different places: a rational administration wing and an organic auditorium. The forms of the latter appear as an echo of the contours of the Finnish landscape. The concept of differentiation within a topological continuum culminated with the Technical College (Teknillinen Korkeakoulu) in Otaniemi (1955–64), where a large fan-shaped aula functions as the central gestalt. As a curiosity, we might mention that the architecture department facades are clad in marble, perhaps as an ironic allusion to the building's aesthetic content. In Aalto's comprehensive production, the Enzo-Gutzeit Building in Helsinki (1959–62) is a rare bird. The task entailed an adaptation to the neoclassical milieu of the Esplanade, and Aalto assumed its rhythms and proportions. The attempt is successful, in part because the new building does not use the old ones as prototypes but instead operates as a modern complement, simultaneously classical and anticlassical.

Though Aalto furthered his conception of architecture until the end, it cannot be ignored that he, like many others who receive too many commissions, lost some of the immediacy that marked his early and mature work. That which should have been living representation became mannered, such as the university building in Jyväskylä and the city center in Seinäjoki. Conversely, his large Finlandia center in Helsinki (1971) holds its own against the National Museum and the Parliament, forming with these a strong group along Töölö Lake. Here the continuity of the Finnish tradition achieves a true "new monumentality."[13]

Aalto's work has become an important source of inspiration for architects of the postwar period. Norway was receptive to his organic functionalism, and the period's leading architects, Knut Knutsen and Arne Korsmo, developed his ideas, each in his own way. Knutsen's aim was the creation of a "modest architecture," which bows to the surroundings, and it was thus natural for him to embrace Aalto's formal destruction. Knutsen's own summer house in Portør (1948) seems thus a pile of planks, hidden away among the rocks; it has been said that one must form a search party to find the house again after going for a swim. Knutsen's pre-ecological concept of architecture was

A. Aalto, Technical College, Otaniemi, Helsinki

A. Aalto, Enzo-Gutzeit Building, Helsinki

A. Aalto, Finlandia Center, Helsinki

A. Aalto, Finlandia Center, Helsinki

A. Aalto, City Hall, Säynätsalo, Finland

K. Lund and N. Slaato, Villa, Lysaker, Oslo

pioneering, and many sought to follow in his footsteps; this can be seen in the establishment of the Wood Prize in 1961, an honor given to those that "with good architecture call forth those values that yet inhabit wood."[14] Knutsen was the first recipient, and among later winners were Kjell Lund and Nils Slaato, who achieved particularly interesting new interpretations of Norwegian typological qualities through the use of differentiated structures with affinities to traditional stave and log construction.

Arne Korsmo charted out other paths. As one of Norway's pioneer functionalists, he wished to further modern architecture and in this connection undertook a study trip to the United States in 1949 to see the work of Frank Lloyd Wright and Ludwig Mies van der Rohe, among others. He was also highly interested in Gropius's method of teaching, and introduced the Bauhaus method in Scandinavia.[15] Korsmo engaged in the domestic in an entirely different way than Knutsen. For Korsmo, it was an issue of renewal, whereby the outer forms of the regional typology would recede for the benefit of more essential interpretations. This is beautifully expressed in his own house in Oslo (1952–55), whose clear construction and open plan are markedly modern, while the interior's lively furnishings and use of color echo old Norwegian farm interiors. In general, it is mood that links Korsmo's interior with the domestic tradition. We will come later to Korsmo's most significant student, Sverre Fehn, but first let us look at the contributions of his postwar collaborator, the Dane Jørn Utzon.

Korsmo and Utzon met in Stockholm after the war and found in each other a common attitude toward architecture and the world. According to Korsmo, this consisted in the desire to "smuggle joy into the logic of the time," or if you will, to recover the "most primitive things." He recalled, "On one of our summer outings—to Sandhamn in the skerries outside Stockholm—we spoke together in just the right way. Everything we found—stones, bits of glass, shiny black coal—we collected into our first poem on our common joy for the spatial experience."[16]

The meeting was the beginning of an extensive collaboration during the postwar years. Among the many unawarded competition projects, the plan for Vestre Vika (1948) in Oslo should be mentioned. The project appears like a living organic structure engaged in the town; thus the project allowed for successive building in both horizontal and vertical directions, preferably by various architects. "It was the particular rise and fall of the terrain, the rhythms of the Oslo landscape, and the resulting dimensioning requirements that lead to this concept."[17] Aalto's influence is notable, but Utzon and Korsmo took one step further toward an open understanding of place.

In the following years, Utzon produced a series of projects that transpose the ideas of the Oslo project to the Danish context. Among these, the housing scheme Birkehøj (1960) is especially noteworthy in that it recaptures the

A. Korsmo, own house in Planetveien, Oslo

K. Knutsen, own summer house, Portør, Norway

traditional identity of place in a new way. Here, adaptation to the terrain and assembly around an urban space are united with an open structure based on theme and variation. Unfortunately, the project was never realized, but his Kingo Houses in Helsingør (1956) and the Fredensborg Houses (1960–64) realize analogous ideas. Both works present a convincing response to the call for a new dwelling that accommodates a given place. As such, the houses are indisputably Danish, while they are also modern and timeless. For timeless here is not an abstraction—that which belongs to no time—but that which is always valid. That is precisely how Utzon's buildings seem: they stand forth as a self-evident and enduring part of the place.

It is in this approach to the timeless that the significance of Utzon's contribution lies. The timeless can be likened to the original; we have already stressed that the origins must be present in any true work of architecture, though without it pretending to be an origin per se. Utzon remains Danish and modern, but at the same time, his work reveals basic architectural principles, opening thereby for further fruitful development. The principles he uses in his competition projects, as well as in the Sydney Opera House, can be characterized as a synthesis of Le Corbusier's "Five Points" and Aalto's organic form. Thus, Utzon defines the elements of building as "podium," and "cover," and between lie the free plan and space organized by the built structure.[18] It is again evident that we are presented with an interpretation of earth, sky, and horizon, an interpretation that is both new and old, and truly essential.

Bagsvaerd Church outside Copenhagen (1973–76) ranks as Utzon's most important Danish work.[19] Here, his basic principles are domesticated, in that both walls and floor are subdued and geometricized in a Danish manner, while motifs resonate like echoes of the land's character: stepped gables, repetitive wall sections, disciplined details. The interior's lateral concrete structure unites modern technology with memories of the traditional, and the consistent bay divisions show how an original building method can be renewed. Over the precise spatial composition and tensive built form hover great vaults, images of the Danish sky; here, space gains another dimension, and the whole thus becomes an explanatory world image.

In the fifties and sixties, Utzon was somewhat alone in renewing Danish architecture, but in the following decades, several significant architects emerged on the scene. Among these, Henning Larsen occupies a special position, as a result of both the quality of his work and of his engagement in contemporary debate; thus, his work established a clear stance with respect to structuralism and postmodernism. Larsen's production is characterized by typical Danish qualities such as order, simplicity, and gentle detailing, such as in his Høje Taastrup High School (1981), where the human scale of the open courtyard forms a natural transition to the soft landscape of the surroundings. In his Commercial College (Handelshøyskolen) in Copenhagen (1988), postmodern motifs are employed outside and inside,

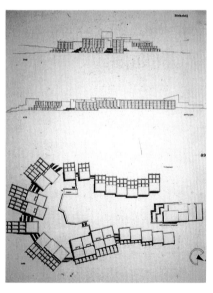

J. Utzon, project for Birkehøj, Denmark

J. Utzon, Bagsværd Church, near Copenhagen

J. Utzon, Fredensborg Houses, northeast Zealand, Denmark

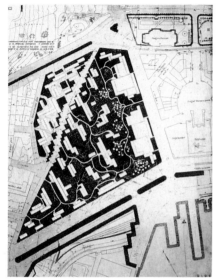

A. Korsmo and J. Utzon, Project for Vestre Vika, Oslo

H. Larsen, School of Economics, Copenhagen

while the whole is organized about symmetrical axes; the result is a distinct gestalt quality that, thanks to the Danish simplicity that marks the complex, does not seem nostalgic. Larsen thus succeeds in showing the possibilities of a new monumentality.

In Sweden, architecture underwent a process of banalization during the postwar years, resulting in bare "reasonable" forms, stripped of any traditional artistic value. This Swedish "empiricism"[20] had its roots in the functionalism of the thirties, which, in conjunction with a cultural policy of equalization, obliterated all meaningful memories. It was Sigurd Lewerentz who was most successful in resuscitating architecture's artistic dimension during this period. After Asplund's early death in 1940, he was a lone representative of creative power in Sweden. It is interesting to note that Lewerentz's intentions found their best expression in churches and crematoriums. This might seem paradoxical at a time when the "new dwelling" occupied the central position, but precisely because housing had been reduced to an empirical problem, Lewerentz and other Nordic architects were forced to show, in churches and chapels, that one does not live by bread alone. This did not, however, entail any religious profession; it instead represented the need to confer the rank of world image upon architecture. Lewerentz met this challenge in a Swedish manner, that is, through a highly sensitive, though somewhat heterogeneous, assemblage of memories, wherein the cohesive vehicle is mood rather than formal composition. In this respect, his work is eminently Nordic. His major works are the St. Mark church in Björkhagen near Stockholm (1956) and the St. Peter church in Klippan in Skåne (1963). Both re-form and reinterpret numerous motifs within a unified mood based on the unitary use of materials. That his works are rooted in an authentic understanding of nature is proved by his chapels for the crematorium compound in Malmö (1943).

In the course of the last decade, Swedish architecture has experienced a more radical renewal, thanks to architects such as Carl Nyrén, Jan Gezelius, and Bengt Lindroos.[21] In particular, Nyrén's church in Gottsunda near Uppsala (1980) is a convincing example of a new interpretation of the Swedish conception of form; it is not only the domestic details, such as the vertical clapboard and applied decoration, that is of import but also the total gestalt, at once new and old. In this way, Nyrén shows that the Swedish identity can yet bear fruit.

The Danish emigré Erik Asmussen holds a special position in the Swedish milieu; as an anthroposophist, he adheres to a view of wholeness based in the metamorphoses of identities, and this approach engages his work in the Nordic and the contemporary. His Rudolf Steiner seminary in Järna, south of Stockholm (after 1970), makes his conception of architecture convincingly manifest. Space, form, and gestalt express that life here takes place, while the anthroposophical vocabulary accommodates the undulant

C. Nyren, Gottsunda Church, near Uppsala, Sweden

S. Lewerenz, Crematorium, Malmö, Sweden

S. Lewerenz, Björkhagen Church, Stockholm

central Swedish landscape, and the details take up traditional Swedish folk motifs. As a whole, the Järna project represents a living alternative to the indifferent settlements of Swedish empiricism.

We have characterized Norway as the most difficult of the Nordic lands. Its traditional typology is assuredly strong and continuous, but it has not lent itself to renewal in our time. Ove Bang suggested one possibility; Korsmo and Knutsen later showed that the Norwegian can still be expressed. For the most part, however, the postwar period has been marked by confusion. As such, the isms have seemed more intrusive than elsewhere in the North, and as a result, the environment has been increasingly affected by placeless prefab houses.[22] The positive contributions to regional modernism that do exist, which include the Wood Prize works, are but drops in the ocean. And it is characteristic that the postwar's most significant architect, Sverre Fehn, has had limited possibilities to realize his ideas; much of what he has built, however, form important stages in the development of Norwegian modernism.

Fehn's conception of architecture was already evident when, in 1952, he wrote an article about a study tour to Morocco: "When one today travels southward, to French Morocco, in order to study primitive architecture, it is no journey to discover new things. One recognizes. Such must be Frank Lloyd Wright's houses . . . such must be Mies van der Rohe's walls."[23] The article is illustrated with plans and sections of settlements in the desert that exhibit the interplay of nature and architecture. Another text reads: "Only by building the new can we achieve a dialogue with the past." Here again, we confront the desire to recover the most primitive things, or if you will, the recognition that the basic principles of architecture are timeless. But the statement also implies that the timeless finds form in time and space, and in his buildings, Fehn shows what this means. His major work, the Hedemark Museum in Hamar (1979) is thus inserted into the ruins of the medieval bishop's quarters, while it is at the same time highly modern. Here, the new and old mutually explain each other. The space is impressed by a strong and articulate construction based on the interplay of wood and concrete. A pronounced Norwegian sense of form is thereby expressed; the project thus confirms that typology does not consist in the mimesis of prototypes but in the reinterpretation of principles.[24] The same sense for the expressive possibilities of construction are the basis for Villa Busk near Brevik (1990), where wood and concrete find new assembly. The house is moreover an unsurpassed study in adaptation to place, and though it uses conventional house forms, it emerges as a self-evident part of the surroundings. It is interesting to note that Fehn here employs "known" elements, such as tower, bridge, and gable. Fehn's Glacier Museum in Fjærland (1991) possesses the same qualities and is an extraordinary essay in the translation of a landscape into architecture by means of basic formal units.

S. Fehn, Villa Busk, Bamble, Norway

S. Fehn, Glacier Museum, Fjærland, Norway

S. Fehn, Hedmarksmuseum, Hamar, Norway

Characteristic differences within the common Nordic attitude come to light by comparing Fehn's work to his contemporary Reima Pietilä's. The latter's work displays an analogous sense for place and basic architectural principles, but whereas Fehn's work is structurally founded, Pietilä's allows the forms themselves to speak. And their speech gathers and expresses the Finnish environment. The architect himself tells that before he began work on the student union building, Dipoli, at Otaniemi near Helsinki (1961–66), he wandered about the site, "in order to experience a tactile understanding of its form," and thereby "nature itself became the artist that represents the genius of the place."[25] Pietilä characterizes this understanding of the situation as "precognitive," a denomination that corresponds to what we have called "fore-conception." Pietilä shows thereby that recovery of the most primitive things cannot occur along logical paths but must be based on the immediate recognition of "the things themselves."[26] But an understanding of place also includes the need to dwell. In Finland, the response to this need is, as we have seen, a cave of wood, and thus the main rooms at Dipoli are formed as a free topological area under an undulating wooden vault. Despite its original formation, the vault is reminiscent of Finland's old churches and therefore offers new insight into the true essence of typology. In its differentiated formation of space, Dipoli acts as a continuation of Aalto's conception of the building as a composition of qualitative places, but Pietilä goes further than his predecessor with respect to poetic realism. Like a great animal, Dipoli breaks forth from the earth between pines and birches and allows us to experience the *tunnelmaa* (mood) of place as a living presence.

Pietilä's other work is characterized by an analogous originality, while it explains the world to which it belongs. The library in Tampere (1986) is formed in the Finnish manner like a skin around a cave, with an oblique (!) cupola as its center. The whole seems as though it is in the process of becoming; it awakens zoomorphic associations. Pietilä's most extensive work is the center in Tampere's suburb Hervanta (after 1987) that includes administrative, commercial, and cultural functions. This series of buildings works together in a way that unites urban and rural qualities. Again, space forms a counterpoint to the surroundings, while the faceted articulation of the walls repeats nature's fragmented continuum. As such, wandering around this center becomes a manifold experience, though without arriving at any final goal, in accordance with the land itself. But this is why it is necessary that central spaces exist where movement may fall to rest. Finnish churches of the past were such places, and such is Pietilä's Kaleva Church in Tampere (1960–66). With respect to both its urban context and its relation to earth and sky, it functions as a goal, but at the same time, the surrounding concave wall panels communicate with the horizon. The tall standing panels are simultaneously cliff, trees, and built form, while the slots between them maintain Finnish cloven light; thus the church represents the space of the forest as an extensive and undefined place. The vertical light openings of the interior take in the surroundings, while the "altar tree" by Pietilä interprets verticality as growth and web. Hence, the Kaleva Church collects the Finnish environment within a gestalt at once old and new and thereby satisfies our current need for monumentality. The church is indeed a masterwork, which brings us closer to the essence of architecture.

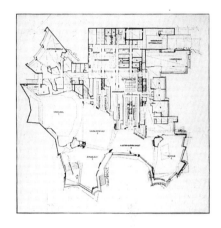

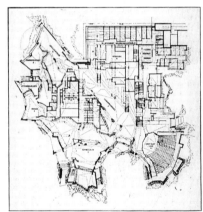

R. Pietilä, Dipoli, Otaniemi, Finland

Our treatment of Nordic architecture has concentrated primarily on single buildings, while the settlement as a whole has remained in the background. This is partly the result of the scatteredness of Northern building groups; and since climate has favored an indoor life, urban space has never been of primary importance. As a result, a true Nordic urbanism, based in appropriate forms, has never arisen.[27] Nonetheless, tun types, village forms, and certain urban complexes have represented an authentic response to the Nordic environment. In particular, Denmark's concentrated population offers much that is of interest, while Stockholm's Gamla Stan holds its own among European historical centers. Certain contributions to the development of urban structures have also been made in Finland and Norway in connection

R. Pietilä, Dipoli, Otaniemi, Finland

R. Pietilä, Hervanta Center, Tampere, Finland

R. Pietilä, Hervanta Center, Tampere, Finland

with their independence movements in the nineteenth century. Helsinki's Senate Square and Christiania's Karl Johan Street are important examples.

A Nordic urbanism that manifests the natural environment that we have taken as a basis for this book is, however, still absent; and the modernist idea of the "green city" has dissolved much of that which did exist. It is not the task here to suggest solutions; our intent is only to point out promising ideas. In our view, the Swedish-English architect Ralph Erskine is alone in attacking this problem at its roots. His projects for subarctic settlements are both new and representative of a Nordic interpretation of place, in terms of limit and density.[28] Erskine's motto, "form follows climate" is basic in this regard, in that he understands climate qualitatively rather than quantitatively. Erskine's approach has led to promising results in connection with single buildings as well, as in his successful Kiruna settlement (after 1961).

Our treatment of the contribution of the Nordic countries to the development of a new regionalism has shown that a rooted architecture can be realized without any loss of dynamism or openness. Indeed, it is the regional qualities that reify openness, whereas international uniformity would get stuck in monomorphism. It is difference that leads us from place to place, and it is recognition of otherness that allows us to understand ourselves. Nordic regional modernism teaches us, therefore, that unity and multiplicity are two sides of the same issue. Unity consists, here, in an overall world of moods, within which each land retains its own identity. As we have seen, this unity lives through history, as a basic tone that lends meaning to individual works. But before we attempt to give a conclusive definition of Nordic unity, it is first necessary to identify the identity of each land in a few terms.

Denmark is characterized by nearness and uniformity. This means that things emerge almost classically as something, and that the whole is cultivated and well ordered. Nevertheless, Nordic light strips things of their true plasticity, subsuming everything within a comprehensive mood. Architecture corresponds through ordered spatial formations and the rhythms of the wall, which creates lengths of unspecified extension. These have their origin in the repetitive bay structure of half-timbering; nonetheless, this structure is not stressed as such but is instead geometrically abstracted. The dimensions are modest and the details careful. Characteristic gestalt are the stepped gables and additive towers. The Danish archetypology can be traced from farmhouses to Renaissance palaces and villas, C. F. Hansen's ascetic classicism, Klint's sensitive traditionalism, and C. F. Møller's cultivated minimalism, to Utzon's essential modernism.

Sweden's environment is characterized by the meeting of many features and in central Svealand by a diversified landscape, but the land as a whole has a clear geographic definition. Architecture expresses these relations, in that Swedish buildings consist as a rule of unitary volumes with applied motifs that may play the role of memories. Its origins are found in

R. Pietilä, Library, Tampere, Finland

R. Pietilä, Kaleva Church, Tampere, Finland

the log construction, but instead of emphasizing the structural elements, the Swedes subsume them within continuous surfaces. Characteristic gestalt are the stocky tower with contrasting finials, the gambrel gable, and the unified hall space. The eclectic Swedish tradition can be traced from folk architecture and the three-room plan, through medieval churches, the powerful castles of the Renaissance and baroque periods, Östberg and Asplund's fanciful inventions to Nyrén's new interpretations.

Finland is the most unified of the Nordic countries. As a land of forests, it is characterized by endless extension, which is emphasized by lack of relief and distinct spaces. To the space of the forest belongs the cloven light that contributes to the impression of incompleteness. Here, architecture has as its main task to create places in the indefinite, and as a result, interiors are of primary significance. They are not, however, isolated from, but rather interplay with, the outdoors. As a result, construction recedes in favor of a free arrangement of forms. Characteristic gestalt are the unifying roof, the freestanding tower, and the cavernous space. Finnish tradition offers more possibilities than the other Nordic lands; nonetheless, a continuity can be traced from medieval stone churches through the wooden churches of the seventeenth and eighteenth centuries, Engel's picturesque compositions, Saarinen and Sonck's vital fantasies, Aalto's organic deconstruction to Pietilä's deeply felt regionalism.

Norway possesses the most complex and dramatic nature in the North. Valleys and fjords cut deeply into its mountain mass, and the coast is accompanied by islands and skerries. In general, the landscape seems a forum for undefinable forces, while light does not achieve its clarification as a whole. Architecture assumes a correspondingly difficult character. Construction must be emphasized here so that built works may represent the surroundings, but precisely because the environment is so indefinite, an ambiguous character is general. Norwegian architecture has, therefore, its origin in the combination of stave and log construction, that is, in skeletal and massive structures. Characteristic of the gestalt are the rhythmically rising spire, the ambiguous loft, and the introvert cottage. Norwegian tradition can be traced from medieval stave churches through folk architecture, national romanticism's dragon style, functionalism's concrete skeletons to Fehn's characteristic symbiosis of wood and masonry.

It may seem that these generalizations are oversimplified and, as such, unable to capture the multiplicity of tradition in each country. They cannot, of course, be comprehensive, but they aim at the attainment of the essentials—that is, that which we immediately recognize as a country's identity, for identity is a reality, despite all deviation from the typical. We recognize it spontaneously; if this were not so, there would be no meaning in visiting other places.[29] The significance of essentials is confirmed by the works themselves. Recognition of identities provides us with guidelines for dealing with the situations of the day, for these require that we renounce the

R. Erskine, project for a subarctic settlement

H. Sohlberg, motif from Røros, Norway

accidental in favor of the rooted, in a sense that expresses our understanding of the given environment. Architecture, in other words, is a form of understanding. As such, it consists in explanation of the unity of life and place, in order that we may understand where we are, how we are, what we are. When successful, architecture becomes the art of building and thereby a representation of an inhabited landscape.

The Nordic art of building manifests the Nordic world. Throughout all variation, this world remains a ground from which all built work arises. We have seen that Nordic light is its most basic quality, and that this light gives presence to an environment: where the web and the thicket emerge in contrast to the South's self-evident sun-space where things stand forth as such. This entails that Nordic inhabitants cannot isolate themselves from things but become drawn into a dialogue with the given; hence, things are not objects but effective forces. In this anticlassical world, architecture has another, nonmimetic task: here, represent does not denote depict but engagement in the web. Thus Nordic built work does not stand as an independent body but opens toward the environment, simultaneously absorbing it within. In architectonic terms, then, Nordic space is topology, Nordic form collage, and Nordic gestalt a hybrid that unites contradictions.[30] And the Nordic dweller is not an observer but a participant. This implies that the building becomes a home, in a way very different from the Southern house. It becomes a place where the function of dwelling is consummated through internal participation.

We have maintained that the Nordic world and Nordic architecture have an essential affinity to our time. Both are characterized by openness, interplay, and dynamism, and modern architecture sought to rid itself of the stylistic dogmatism of the past. (That this entails a certain misunderstanding of the concept of style is another issue.) The new freedom was not understood as something absolute but as the recovery of the origins: only in this way may we resist the devaluation of values.[31] Regionalism is the second phase of this process of recovery, and Nordic architecture comes therefore into the center of interest. In the Nordic world, the origins live on, despite all confusion and foolishness, and the regional modernism of the North shows us that change does not exclude that the origins remain.

Kalundborg

Chapter 1

1. W. Hellpach, *Geopsyche: Die Menschenseele unter dem Einfluss von Wetter und Klima* (Stuttgart, 1977) (1911).

2. K. Varnedoe, *Northern Light: Realism and Symbolism in Scandinavian Painting 1880–1910* (Brooklyn, 1982).

3. R. S. Wurman, *What Will Be Has Always Been: The Words of Louis I. Kahn* (New York, 1986), 216.

4. G. d'Annunzio, *Laudi del Cielo, del Mare, della Terra e degli Ero* (Rome, 1933).

5. The most magnificent expression of sun-space is Bernini's St. Peter's Square.

6. For example, the work of Carlo Carrà in the 1920s.

7. The baroque *teatrum sacrum* is a part of this context.

8. The cultures of the South are thus "stone cultures," whereas those of the North are "wood cultures."

9. S. Giedion, *Space, Time and Architecture* (Cambridge, Mass., 1967) (1941), 622.

10. From the Danish national song.

11. O. F. Bollnow, *Unruhe und Geborgenheit im Weltbild neuerer Dichter* (Stuttgart, 1953), 234.

12. Thus the German edition of Olavus Magnus's Nordic history was entitled *Historien der Mitternächtigen Länder* (Basel, 1596).

13. Heidegger calls the path *Holzweg,* and writes, "Holz lautet ein alter Name für Wald. Im Holz sind Wege, die meist verwachsen jäh im Unbegangenen aufhören. Sie heissen Holzwege." M. Heidegger, *Holzwege* (Frankfurt am Main, 1950).

14. A. de Saint-Exupéry, *Citadelle* (Paris, 1948).

15. V. Scully, *The Earth, the Temple and the Gods* (New Haven, 1962).

16. U. Ehrensvärd, *Den svenska tomten* (Stockholm, 1979).

17. *Kalevala,* translated by W. F. Kirby (London, 1985) (1907).

18. *Kalevala,* Runo 3.

19. *Kalevala,* Runo 50.

20. *Tapiola* is a symphonic poem about the god of the forest, Tapio. Op. 112, composed 1926.

21. R. Nasgaard, *The Mystic North* (Toronto, 1984), 110.

22. Ø. Parmann, *Halfdan Egedius* (Oslo, 1979), 69.

23. T. Martin, D. Sivén, *Akseli Gallén-Kallela* (Helsinki, 1985).

24. K. Varnedoe, *Nordisk gullalderkunst* (Oslo, 1987), 72.

25. P. Vad, *Hammershøi* (Copenhagen, 1990), 200.

26. Cited in O. F. Bollnow, *Rilke* (Stuttgart, 1951), 108.

27. *Duino Elegies,* translated by A. Poulin Jr. (Boston, 1977), 65.

28. M. Heidegger, *Hebel der Hausfreund* (Pfullingen, 1957), 13.

29. "Representation" corresponds to the Greek *mimesis,* while "complementation" is a creative, "romantic" activity.

30. Thus Serlio called the rusticated wall *opera di natura.*

31. S. Giedion, "Über den neuen Regionalismus," *Architektur und Gemeinschaft* (Hamburg, 1956), 84ff.

32. W. Worringer, *Formprobleme der Gotik.* Munich, 1907, and *Griechtum und Gotik* (Munich, 1928).

33. We might also mention German-Austrian classical music, and German philosophy in general, represent a synthesis of a similar kind. Thus Heidegger is but the last representative of the desire to enjoin Greek "presence" and the Nordic "way," as an attempt to better understand that which "is."

34. Cf. Bernini's famous critique of Borromini's "Nordic" buildings as "an architecture for monsters." *Tagebuch des Herrn von Chantelou über die Reise des Cavaliere Bernini nach Frankreich* (20. 10. 1665) (Munich, 1919), 354.

35. H. W. Ahlmann, "Sveriges förhållande til omvärlden." *Sverige, land och folk* (Stockholm, 1954), 1.

36. J. Roosval, *Den baltiska Nordens kyrkor* (Uppsala, 1923).

37. This picturesque quality is typical of Russian architecture. H. Faensen, V. Ivanov, *Early Russian Architecture* (London, 1972).

38. E. Cassirer, *Philosophie der Symbolischen Formen* II (Berlin, 1923–1929).

1. But neither map nor perspective can capture the mood of the place.

2. The same is true of the Balkans and the Iberian peninsula.

3. K. Sønderby, O. Gelstad, A. Marcus, J. Paludan, J. Smith, and M. Stage, *Det danske landet* (Copenhagen, n.d.), 36.

4. Ibid., 95.

5. Ibid., 247.

6. C. Norberg-Schulz, "Jørn Utzon: Church at Bagsværd." *Global Architecture* 61 (Tokyo, 1981).

7. E. M. R. Mandt, *Historisk Beskrivelse over Øvre Tellemarke* (Copenhagen 1777), re-issued Espa, 1989.

8. Bjørnstjerne Bjørnson, "Over de høie fjælde."

9. Christian Krohg called the mountains in Lofoten "altars for the gods of loneliness." L. Ryvarden, *Lofoten og Vesteråle* (Oslo, 1981).

10. Both Nidaros and Trondheim were used in the Middle Ages, but the name of the bishopric was Nidaros. From the late Middle Ages onward, Trondheim became common.

11. E. van Mingroot and E. van Ermen, *Norge og Norden i gamle kart og trykk* (Oslo, 1988), 57.

12. As, for example, in Kviteseid.

13. T. Vesaas, "Telemark," in *Huset og fuglen* (Oslo, 1971), 176.

14. C. Norberg-Schulz, "Fjell," in *Minnesjord* (Oslo, 1991), 19.

15. K. E. Johnson, "Bilder fra Nord-Norge." Parmann, op. cit. p, 190.

16. Along the coast, one finds villages in Norway too.

17. C. Norberg-Schulz, *Intentions in Architecture* (London, 1963).

18. H. Vreim, "Trekk av byggeskikkens geografi i Norge." *Forening til norske fortids-minnesmerkers bevaring,* year book, 1936.

19. Stockholm was founded in the mid-1200s.

20. *Sverige, land och folk* (Stockholm, 1954. vol. 2), 718.

21. Ibid., 718, 720.

22. "Dalarne," says R. Dybeck, "is like Sweden in summary, hills, dales, forests, fields, lakes and rivers are there combined and incorporated; and therein lies its renown natural distinctiveness." Cited from H. Hofberg, *Genom Sveriges bygde* (Stockholm 1868), 177.

23. Until 1658, Norway and Denmark nearly met at the issue of the Göta River.

24. We intend nothing derogatory with the word "eclectic."

25. E. Lundberg, *Svensk bostad* (Stockholm, 1978), 195ff.

26. *Sverige, land och folk,* vol. I, 181.

27. Such as Gunnar Asplund and Sigurd Lewerentz.

28. T. Suominen, and M. A. Pitkänen, *Det finländska landskapet* (Espoo, 1977).

29. O. Okkonen, *Finsk konst* (Porvoo and Helsinki, 1946), 6.

30. Cited from R. Layton, *Sibelius* (London, 1965), 78.

31. The expression is Reima Pietilä's.

32. S. Giedion, "The New Regionalism," *Architecture You and Me* (Cambridge, Mass., 1958).

33. The Italian word *veduta* means "something seen."

Chapter 3

1. C. Norberg-Schulz, M. Suzuki, and Y. Futagawa, *Wooden Houses* (New York, 1979).

2. "Fore-conception" (*Vorverständnis*) as an expression of man's way of being in the world is Heidegger's. See M. Heidegger, *Grundfragen der Philosophie* (Frankfurt am Main, 1984) (1937–38).

3. M. Heidegger, "Erst Gebild wahrt Gesicht," *Aus der Erfahrung des Denkens* (Pfullingen, 1954), 13.

4. As we shall see later, the Norwegian *loft* is a characteristic example.

5. J. Trier, "First," *Nachrichten von der Gesellschaft der Wissenschaften zu Göttingen,* phil.-hist. Klasse IV, N. F. III. 4, 1940, 55.

6. J. Trier, "Irminsul," *Westfalische Forschungen,* IV (Münster, 1941), 101.

7. Trier, "First," 117.

8. Ibid., 56.

9. Others include "wall," akin to Latin *vallis,* "valley," "floor," akin to *field,* both derived from protoindoeuropean *pele-*[2] to spread.

10. This view of wholeness echoes in the word "ecology," which is derived from Greek *oikos,* "house."

11. J. Trier, "Giebel," *Zeitschrift für deutsches Altertum und deutsche Literatur* (Brussels, 1939), 22.

12. The classical *tympanum* should not be mistaken for a gable.

13. The characteristic trees of the South (pine, cypress, and palm) seem primarily whole things, with definite character.

14. Thus the German word for half-timbering is *Fachwerk.*

15. Norberg-Schulz, Suzuki, Futagawa, *op.cit.*

16. *Bulhus* construction is perfected on Gotland. See J. K. Christiansen, *Lunderhagestugan* (Bunge, 1988).

17. P. Brogaard, H. Lund, and H. E. Nørregaard-Nielsen, *Landbrugets huse* (Copenhagen, 1980), 45.

18. For more about Danish building methods, see B. Stoklund, *Bondegård og byggeskik* (Copenhagen, 1969).

19. C. Elling, *Det klassiske København* (Copenhagen, 1944), 5, 78.

20. R. Hauglid, *Laftekunst* (Oslo, 1980); and G. Boethius, *Studier i den nordiska timmerbyggnadskonsten* (Stockholm, 1927).

21. E. Lundberg, *Svensk bostad* (Stockholm, 1978), 204ff.

22. P. A. Mårdh, *Röda Stugor* (Stockholm, 1990).

23. For the development of the Swedish cottage, see S. Erixon, *Svensk byggnadskultur* (Stockholm, 1947).

24. Mårdh, *Röda Stugor,* 4.

25. N. E. Wickberg, *Byggnadkonst i Finland* (Helsinki, 1959), 16; and P. Sihvo, *Tradition und Volkskunst in Finnland* (Helsinki, 1978).

26. Wickberg, *Byggnadkonst* 20, 56–57.

27. Such as Sonck's own house on Åland, "Lasses Villa," from 1895. *Lars Sonck architect 1870–1956* (Helsinki, 1981), 14 ff.

28. G. Bugge, C. Norberg-Schulz, *Stav og laft i Norge* (Oslo, 1969).

29. The Norwegian word for this smoke vent is *ljore,* derived from *ljor,* meaning either, "opening in the clouds, clearing" or "hole or tear in a tree, or sore on the back of a horse." See Falk, Torp, *Etymologisk Ordbog over det hozske og det danske sprog* (Oslo, 1991), "ljore," p. 465.

30. H. Vreim, "Trekk av byggeskikkens geografi i Norge." *Forening til norske fortidsminnesmerkers bevaring,* yearbook, 1936.

31. Bugge, Norberg-Schulz, *Stav og laft,* 27.

32. Ibid., p 29, 133 ff.

33. R. Hauglid et al., *Byborgerens hus i Norge* (Oslo, 1963).

34. D. Rognlien, ed. *Treprisen, Thirteen Prize-winning Norwegian Architects* (Oslo, 1988).

35. In this way, Hans Sedlmayr sees art as "*die Darstellung eines anschaulichen Charakters*" (the representation of an imageable character). "Ursprung und Anfänge der Kunst," *Epochen und Werke* 1. (Vienna-Munich, 1959), 7.

Chapter 4

1. V. Scully, *The Earth, the Temple and the God* (New Haven, 1962).

2. C. Norberg-Schulz, *Genius Loci* (London and New York, 1980), 78ff.

3. This fore-conception is thus not the result of a process of "socialization," but is instead given as a "timeless" structure of the human constitution.

4. K. Lynch, *The Image of the City* (Cambridge, Mass., 1960).

5. M. A. Hansen, *Orm og Tyr* (Copenhagen, 1959), 377.

6. M. Eliade, *Das Heilige und das Profane* (Hamburg, 1957), 20, 27.

7. C. Norberg-Schulz, *Meaning in Western Architecture* (London, 1975) chap. 4.

8. Such is S. Sabina in Rome, from 422.

9. An attempt has been made in Norberg-Schulz, *Genius Loci.*

10. E. Lundberg, *Byggnadskonsten i Sverige under medeltiden 1000–1400* (Stockholm, 1940), 124 ff.

11. T. Littmarck, *Gamla Uppsala* (Uppsala, 1985).

12. Petäjavesi is not medieval; it was built 1763–1775. See L. Petterson, *Finnish Wooden Church* (Helsinki, 1989), 83.

13. An example is Troudheim Cathedral, where a tall spike was erected over the crossing following the fire of 1531.

14. It is commonly supposed that churches were built on or near pagan cult sites.

15. Hansen, *Orm og Tyr,* 278ff.

16. The "stave churches" from Hemse and Gotland are thus more closely related to sleppvegg construction than to Norwegian stave construction. Continental wooden churches are, as far as we can see, a combination of high-strip and half-timbered constructions.

17. The term "lace collar" (*kniplingskrave*) is taken from G. Bugge, *Stavkirkene i Norge* (Oslo, 1981), 10.

18. R. Hauglid, *Norske stavkirke* (Oslo, 1976), 296.

19. G. Boethius, *Hallar, tempel och stavkyrko* (Stockholm, 1931).

20. R. Hauglid, *Norske stavkirke* (Oslo, 1969), 1.

21. See Bugge, *Stavkirkene i Norge.*

22. E. Lundberg, "Domkyrkobygget i Lund." *Konsthistorisk tidsskrift* nr. 1, 1965.

23. N. E. Wickberg, *Byggnadskonst i Finland* (Helsinki, 1959), 12.

24. J. Baum, *Romanische Baukunst in Frankreich* (Stuttgart, 1928).

25. W. Horn, "On the Origins of the Medieval Bay System," *Journal of the Society of Architectural Historians* 17, no. 2, (1958).

26. W. Horn, and E. Born, *The Barns of the Abbey of Beaulieu and the Granges of Coxwell and Beaulieu-St. Leonards* (Berkeley and Los Angeles, 1965).

27. W. Worringer, *Formprobleme der Gotik* (Munich, 1930), 68.

28. Lundberg, "Domkyrkobygget i Lund."

29. In great evidence in the Durham Cathedral, built 1093–1133.

30. J. Roosval, *Den baltiska Nordens kyrkor* (Uppsala, 1924), 65.

31. An example of this is Stavanger Cathedral.

32. M. Mackeprang, *Vore Landsbykirker* (Copenhagen, 1944).

33. Lundberg, *Byggnadskonsten,* 1940, 134ff.

34. An acknowledgement which dates back to, among others, K. F. Schinkel.

35. Lundberg, *Byggnadskonsten,* 1940, 486ff.

36. L. Huovinen, *Åbo Domkyrka* (Turku, 1980).

37. G. Fischer, *Domkirken i Trondheim* (Oslo, 1965).

38. K. J. Conant, *Early Medieval Church Architecture* (Baltimore, 1942).

39. This was unfortunately not understood when the remaining parts of the west front were designed.

Chapter 5

1. The postmodernism of the 1980s was also marked by classical forms.

2. The expression is S. Giedion's.

3. V. Lorenzen, *Christian IVs Byanlæg og Bygningsarbejde* (Copenhagen, 1937).

4. Both as a "play of forces" (the bearing and the borne) and as "being in space."

5. This concept is "classically" formulated by Plato.

6. E. Forssman, *Dorisch, Jonisch, Korintisch* (Uppsala, 1961).

7. This concept was systematized by Serlio in the sixteenth century.

8. Alberti's well-known definition of harmony is that nothing can be added nor taken away without it being "for the worse."

9. C. Norberg-Schulz, *Meaning in Western Architecture* (London, 1975).

10. E. Forssman, *Säule und Ornament* (Stockholm, 1956), 32.

11. J. A. Skovgaard, *A King's Architecture* (London, 1973), 7, 67.

12. Lorenzen, *Christian IVs Byanlæg.*

13. Cited from E. Cornell, *Ragnar Östberg, svensk arkitekt* (Stockholm, 1965), 218ff.

14. R. Josephson, *Tessin* (Stockholm, 1930). Tessin the Elder emigrated from Stralsund in 1636, at the age of twenty-one.

15. See H. O. Andersson and Fredric Bedoire, *Stockholms byggnader* (Stockholm, 1977).

16. Josephson, *Tessin.*

17. Josephson, *Tessin,* vol. II, 177.

18. C. Norberg-Schulz, *Baroque Architecture* (New York, 1972).

19. The baroque interpretation of homogeneous space was developed by Guarino Guarini. See C. Norberg-Schulz, *Baroque Architecture.*

20. The enclosing perspective is undoubtedly inspired by Borromini's "colonnade" in the Palazzo Spada in Rome.

21. Josephson, *Tessin,* vol. II, 177.

22. See F. Weilbach, *Lauritz Thura* (Copenhagen, 1924); and K. Voss, *Arkitekten Nicolai Eigtved* (Copenhagen, 1971).

23. See also S. E. Rasmussen, *Byer og bygninger* (Copenhagen, 1949).

24. After the royal palace Christianborg burnt in 1794, the Amalienborg residences were bought by the royal family, who still use them.

25. See K. Voss, *Arkitekten Nicolai Eigtved.* The church was built on a reduced plan by Ferdinand Meldahl, 1876–1894.

26. See C. Norberg-Schulz, "Der Himmel als Seinsweise," in *Neresheim* (Berlin, 1992).

27. Eighteenth-century Norwegian church architecture still lacks an exhaustive presentation.

28. Also in Sweden, there were built numerous wooden churches. See E. Nordin, *Svenska träkyrkor* (Stockholm, 1965).

29. Before the Second World War, it was common to call the time after the Middle Ages "the newer time." Finnish wooden churches are collected in L. Petterson, *Finnish Wooden Church* (Helsinki, 1989).

30. C. Norberg-Schulz, "Jarand Rønjom som kirkebygger," *Kunst og Kultur,* no. 1, 1986.

31. C. Norberg-Schulz, *Late Baroque and Rococo Architecture* (New York, 1974).

32. E. Kaufmann, *Von Ledoux bis Le Corbusier* (Vienna, 1933).

33. C. Norberg-Schulz, *Late Baroque,* E. Kaufmann, "Three Revolutionary Architects, Boullée, Ledoux and Lequeu," *Transactions of the American Philosophical Society* (Philadelphia, October, 1952).

34. The typology was banalized by J. N. L. Durand.

35. C. M. Smidt, *Vor Frue Kirke* (Copenhagen, 1980).

36. Aslaksby in collaboration with U. Hamran, *Arkitektene Christian Grosch og Karl Friedrich Schinkel og byggingen av Det Kongelige Frederiks Universitet i Christiania* (Øvre Ervik, 1986).

37. N. E. Wickberg, *Carl Ludwig Engel* (Berlin, 1970). Also N. E. Wickberg, *Senaatintori* (Rungsted Kyst, 1981).

38. The changes were designed by Engel's successor, E. B. Lohrmann.

39. *Um 1800* is the title of a book by Paul Mebes (Munich, 1918) that gives a good overview of European classicism around 1800.

Chapter 6

1. W. Blaser, *Fantasie in Holz* (Basel, 1987).

2. "Swiss-style" houses appear already in park complexes from the end of the eighteenth century. See W. Blaser, *Bauernhaus der Schweiz* (Basel, 1983). *Einführung* by H. -R. Heyer.

3. Although women did not receive suffrage before 1971!

4. C. Norberg-Schulz, *Einführung* in Blaser, *Fantasie in Holz.*

5. V. Scully, *The Shingle Style and the Stick Style* (New Haven, 1971), lix.

6. E. Sundt, *Om Renlighets-Stellet i Norge* (Christiania, 1969).

7. Scully, *The Shingle Style,* 162.

8. Norway had been under Danish rule since 1380.

9. Of essential importance was the publication of Asbjørnson and Moe's *Norwegian Folk Tales* in 1841.

10. A. K. Pihl Atmer, *Sommarnöjet i skärgårde* (Stockholm, 1987).

11. B. Grandien, *Rönndruvans glöd* (Stockholm, 1987), 17ff.

12. Ibid., 74ff.

13. Ibid., 267ff.

14. The room today is at the Norwegian Folk Museum in Oslo.

15. S. Tschudi-Madsen, *Henrik Bull* (Oslo, 1983).

16. K. E. Granath, U. Hård af Segerstad, *Carl Larssongården* (Stockholm, 1979).

17. Mario Praz has called such a home "a museum of the soul."

18. B. Romare, *Verk av L. I. Wahlman* (Lund, 1954).

19. B. Palm, *Arkitekten Carl Westman* (Lund, 1954), 200.

20. E. Cornell, *Ragnar Östberg svensk arkitekt* (Stockholm, 1965).

21. That is, ten years after the death of Klint; the complex was finished by his son Kaare Klint.

22. The statement is Louis Kahn's. See R. S. Wurman, *What Will Be Has Always Been* (New York, 1986).

23. C. Norberg-Schulz, "Fra nasjonalromatikk til funksjonalisme," *Norges Kunsthistorie,* vol. 6 (Oslo, 1983), 29ff.

24. S. Ringbom, *Stone, Style and Truth* (Helsinki, 1987).

25. Armas Lindgren's house was later destroyed by fire.

26. A. Christ-Janer, *Eliel Saarinen* (Chicago, 1979), 135.

27. *Lars Sonck 1870–1956* (Helsinki, 1981).

28. In Norway, classicism reappeared in Henrik Bull's buildings for the Jubilee Exhibition in Christiania in 1914.

29. C. Norberg-Schulz, "Fra nasjonalromatikk," 45.

30. The expression is Lars Backer's.

31. S. E. Rasmussen, *Nordische Baukunst* (Berlin, 1940), 98.

32. Stockholm's Enskilda Bank was published by Gregor Paulsson in the forward-looking book *Den nya arkitekturen* (Stockholm, 1916).

33. C. Caldenby, O. Hultin, *Asplund* (Stockholm, 1985).

34. H. Hals, *Fra Christiania til Stor Oslo* (Oslo, 1929).

35. The examples are numerous, let us just name the Österbotten cities: Vasa, Kristiinankaupunki, Uusikaarlepyy, Pietersaari, Kaarlepyy, Kaskinen.

36. G. Schildt, *Det vita bordet* (Helsinki, 1982).

37. The latter is the case in Norway today.

38. S. Giedion, *Spätbarocker und romantischer Klassizismus* (Munich, 1922).

Chapter 7

1. W. Gropius, *Internationale Architektur* (Munich, 1925), 7.

2. H. -R. Hitchcock and P. Johnson, *The International Style* (New York, 1932), 20. "The idea of style as the frame of potential growth, rather than a fixed and crushing mould, has developed with the recognition of underlying principles."

3. S. Giedion, *Architecture, You and Me* (Cambridge, Mass., 1958), 26.

4. C. Norberg-Schulz, "Det nye tradisjon," *Kunst og kultur* 1, 1991.

5. Le Corbusier, *Oeuvre complète, 1910–29* (Zurich, 1937), 128.

6. C. Norberg-Schulz, *Roots of Modern Architecture* (Tokyo, 1988).

7. Thus, it was "forbidden" to use such motifs as pitched roofs, arches, gables, or "hole" windows.

8. Le Corbusier's geometric conception of the architectonic gestalt is already evident in *Towards a New Architecture* (Paris, 1923), 128.

9. Le Corbusier, "Fünf Punkte zu einer neuen Architektur." A. Roth, *Zwei Wohnhäuser von Le Corbusier und Pierre Jeanneret* (Stuttgart, 1927), 7.

10. L. Backer, "Skansen," *Byggekunst,* (1925), 129.

11. U. Åhrén, "Brytningar," *Svenska slöjdföreningens årsbok,* 1925.

12. G. Asplund, W. Gahn, S. Markelius, G. Paulsson, E. Sundahl, U. Åhrén, *acceptera* (Stockholm, 1931).

13. *Nordisk functionalism,* G. Lundahl, ed. (Stockholm, 1980).

14. Asplund et al., *acceptera,* 198.

15. The expression is from *Funktionalismens genombrott och kris,* H. O. Andersson, ed. (Stockholm, 1976).

16. G. Eliassen, *Norske hus* (Oslo, 1959), 325.

17. Giedion later called this simplification "Swedish empiricism."

18. *Lars Backer* (Oslo, 1930).

19. See also C. Norberg-Schulz, *Modern Norwegian Architecture* (Oslo, 1986).

20. G. Blakstad and H. Munthe-Kaas, *Arkitekt Ove Bang* (Oslo, 1943).

21. C. Norberg-Schulz, *Arne Korsmo* (Oslo, 1986).

22. The exhibition was carried out in collaboration with Knut Knutsen and Andreas Nygaard; planning began in 1935.

23. E. Rudberg, *Sven Markelius, arkitekt* (Stockholm, 1989), 32ff.

24. Ibid., 59.

25. B. Linn, *Osvald Almqvist* (Stockholm, 1967).

26. A. Roth, *La nouvelle architecture* (Zurich, 1940).

27. Asplund, quoted by Elias Cornell in *Asplund,* C. Caldenby and O. Hultin, eds. (Stockholm, 1985), 31.

28. S. Wrede, *The Architecture of Erik Gunnar Asplund* (Cambridge, Mass., 1980), 189ff.

29. R. M. Rilke, *Duineser Elegien IX.*

30. The expression "the new tradition" was used by S. Giedion as the subtitle for his book *Space, Time and Architecture* (Cambridge, Mass., 1941).

31. G. Schildt, *Moderna tider. Alvar Aaltos møte med funktionalisme* (Stockholm, 1985), 48.

32. T. Faber, *Dansk arkitektur* (Copenhagen, 1963), 177, 219.

33. J. Pedersen, *Arne Jacobsen* (Copenhagen, 1957).

34. Faber, *Dansk arkitektur*, 210 ff.

35. M. Steinmann, *CIAM, Dokumente, 1928–39* (Basel, 1979). The congress in Frankfurt, 1929, was titled, *Die Wohnung für das Existenzminimum;* Brussels, 1930: *Rationelle Bebauungsweisen;* Athens, 1933: *Die Funktionelle Stadt;* and Paris, 1937: *Wohnung und Erholung.*

36. Asplund et al., *acceptera*, 54.

37. Rudberg, *Sven Markelius*, 140ff.

38. S. Giedion, "The Regional Approach," *Architectural Record,* January, 1954. Later republished in *Architektur und Gemeinschaft* (Hamburg, 1956).

Chapter 8

1. C. Norberg-Schulz, *New World Architecture* (New York, 1988).

2. C. Norberg-Schulz, *Meaning in Western Architecture* (London, New York, 1975), chap. 12.

3. S. Giedion, *Architecture, You and Me* (Cambridge, Mass., 1958).

4. C. Norberg-Schulz, "Henning Larsen, arkitekt," *Et sted å være* (Oslo, 1986).

5. On Islamic architecture in general, see C. Norberg-Schulz, "The Architecture of Unity," *Architecture Education in the Islamic World.* The Aga Khan Awards, 1986.

6. Quoted from M. Heidegger, *Die Kunst und der Raum* (Einsiedln, 1969), 13. "Es ist nicht immer nötig, dass das Wahre sich verkörpere; schon genug, wenn es geistlig umherschwebt und Übereinstimmung bewirkt, wenn es wie Glockenton ernstfreundlich durch die Lüfte wogt."

7. As has Manfredo Tafuri.

8. R. Venturi, *Complexity and Contradiction in Architecture* (New York, 1966).

9. B. Tschumi, *Questions of Space* (London, 1990).

10. C. Norberg-Schulz, "Kahn, Heidegger and the Language of Architecture," *Oppositions* 18 (New York, 1979). Also, C. Norberg-Schulz, "Heidegger's Thinking on Architecture," *Perspecta* 20 (New Haven, 1985).

11. C. Norberg-Schulz, *Modern Norwegian Architecture* (Oslo, 1986), 35ff.

12. In this respect, schematism and confusion (chaos) are two sides of the same coin.

13. *Alvar Aalto, Volume III,* Projekte und Letzte Bauten (Zurich, 1979), 188ff.

14. D. Rognlien, ed., *Treprisen, 1961–1968* (Oslo, 1988), 222.

15. At an internordic seminar at the Statens Håndverks og Kunstindustriskole (SHKS) in Oslo, summer 1952.

16. C. Norberg-Schulz, *Arne Korsmo* (Oslo, 1986), 65.

17. Ibid., 67.

18. J. Utzon, "Platforms and Plateaus," *Zodiac* 10 (Milano, 1962).

19. C. Norberg-Schulz, *Church at Bagsværd* (Tokyo, 1981).

20. The expression is S. Giedion's.

21. C. Norberg-Schulz, *Scandinavia.* Architettura, gli ultimi vent' anni (Milan, 1990).

22. The place-foreign is expressed in type designations such as "Tyrol house," among others.

23. S. Fehn, "Marokansk primitiv arkitektur," *Byggekunst* (1952), 73ff.

24. P. O. Fjeld, *Sverre Fehn: The Thought of Construction* (New York, 1983).

25. R. Pietilä, "Genius Loci: Personal Interpretations," *Genius Loci: A Search for Local Identity* (Helsinki, 1982).

26. The demand for a return to the "things themselves" is due to Edmund Husserl, "the father of phenomenology."

27. The creation of spaces is for the most part appropriated from Middle Europe and the South.

28. "Arctic Architect," in "Ralph Erskine," *Architectural Design* 11–12 (1977), 783ff.

29. Recognition of identities is based in fore-conception.

30. Borromini was the first to use the "hybrid" gestalt.

31. C. Norberg-Schulz, *Roots of Modern Architecture* (Tokyo, 1988).

Alvar Aalto. Projekte und Bauten 1–3. Zurich 1963, 1971, 1979.

(Ahlberg, Hakon, ed.): *Gunnar Asplund, arkitekt.* Stockholm 1943.

Ahlin, J. *Sigurd Lewerentz, arkitekt.* Stockholm 1985.

Ahrens, C.: *Frühe Holzkirchen in nördlichen Europa.* Hamburg 1982.

Andersson, A. *The Art of Scandinavia 2.* London 1968.

Andersson, H. O., Bedoire, F. *Svensk arkitektur. Stockholm 1986.*

Andersson, H. O., ed. *Funktionalismens genombrott och kris.* Stockholm 1976.

Andersson, H. O., ed. *Classicismo nordico.* Milan 1988.

Anker, P. *The Art of Scandinavia 1.* London 1969.

Aslaksby, T. *Arkitektene Christian Heinrich Grosch og Karl Friedrich Schinkel og byggingen av Det Kongelige Frederiks Unviersitet i Christiania.* Øvre Ervik 1986.

Asplund, G., Gahn, W., Markelius, S., Paulsson, G., Sundahl, E., Åhrén, U. *acceptera.* Stockholm 1931.

Lars Backer. Samlede arbeider. Oslo 1930.

Balslev Jørgensen, L. *Danmarks arkitektur. Enfamiliehuset.* Copenhagen 1979.

Balslev Jørsensen, L., Lund, H., Nørregaard-Nielsen, H. E. *Danmarks arkitektur. Magtens bolig.* Copenhagen 1980.

Berg, K. et al. *Norges Kunsthistorie I–VII.* Oslo 1981–83.

Berg, A. *Norske gardstun.* Oslo 1968.

Bjerke, G. *Landsbybebyggelsen i Norge 1.* Oslo 1950.

Blakstad, G., Munthe-Kaas, H. *Arkitekt Over Bang.* Oslo 1943.

Boëthius, G. *Studier i den nordiska timmerbyggnadskonsten.* Stockholm 1927.

————. *Hallar, tempel och stavkyrkor.* Stockholm 1931.

Brogaard, P., Lund, H., Nørregaard-Nielsen, H. E.: *Danmarks arkitektur. Landbrugets huse.* Copenhagen 1980.

Bugge, G. *Stavkirkene i Norge.* Oslo 1981.

Bugge, G., Norberg-Schulz, C. *Stav og laft i Norge.* Oslo 1969.

Byborgerens hus i Norge. Oslo 1963.

Caldenby, C., Hultin, O. *Asplund.* Stockholm 1985.

Caldenby, C., Walldén, Å. *Jan Gezelius.* Stockholm 1989.

Christensen, J. K. *Lunderhagestugan.* Visby 1988.

Christ-Janer, A. *Eliel Saarinen.* Chicago 1979.

Coldevin, A. *Norske storgårder I-II.* Oslo 1950.

Cornell, E. *Ragnar Östberg, svensk arkitekt.* Stockholm 1965.

Cornell, H. *Den svenska konstens historia.* Stockholm 1944.

Dietrichson, L. *De norske stavkirker.* Kristiania og København 1892.

Dietrichson, L., Munthe, H. *Die Holzbaukunst Norwegens.* Berlin 1893.

Eliassen, G. *Norske hus.* Oslo 1950.

Elling, C. *Det klassiske København.* Copenhagen 1944.

————. *Danske borgerhuse.* Copenhagen 1943.

————. *Danske herregaarde.* Copenhagen 1948.

Erixon, S. *Svensk byggnadskultur.* Stockholm 1947.

Faber, T. *Dansk arkitektur.* Copenhagen 1963.

Fischer, G. *Domkirken i Stavanger.* Oslo 1964.

————. *Domkirken i Trondheim I-II.* Oslo 1965.

Fjeld, P. O. *Sverre Fehn. The Thought of Construction.* New York 1983.

Grandien, B. *Rönndruvans glöd.* Stockholm 1987.

Grønvold, U. *Lund & Slaatto.* Oslo 1988.

Hals, H. *Fra Christianis til Stor-Oslo.* Oslo 1929.

Hansen, M. A. *Orm og tyr.* Copenhagen 1959.

Hartmann, S. Villadsen, V.: *Danmarks arkitektur. Byens huse, byens plan.* Copenhagen 1979.

Hauglid, R. *Norske stavkirker I-II.* Oslo 1976. *Laftekunst.* Oslo 1980.

Hausen, M. *Saarinen in Finland.* Helsinki 1989.

Hausen, M., Mikkola, K., Amberg, A. L., Valto, T. *Eliel Saarinen.* Hamburg 1990.

Herrmans, R. *Slott och herremans hus.* Stockholm 1985.

Hvidtfeldt, J. *Den danske bondegård.* Odense 1965.

Härö, E., Kaila, P. *Österbottengården.* Vasa 1978.

Haastrup, U. *Danske kalkmalerier.* Copenhagen 1989.

Johannsen, H., Smidt, C. M. *Danmarks arkitektur. Kirkens huse.* Copenhagen 1981.

Josephson, R. *Tessin I-II.* Stockholm 1930.

Kidder Smith, G. E. *Sweden builds.* London 1957.

Langberg, H. *Danmarks bygningskultur I-II.* Copenhagen 1955.

Lassen, E., Hansen, P., Knudsen, N. A. *Huse i Danmark.* Copenhagen 1942.

Linn, B. *Osvald Almqvist.* Stockholm 1967.

Lorenzen, V. *Christian IVs Byanlæg og Bygningsarbejder.* Copenhagen 1937.

———. *Dansk arkitektur gennem 20 aar.* Copenhagen 1902.

Lund, N. O. *Nordisk arkitektur.* Copenhagen 1991.

Lundahl, G., ed. *Nordisk funktionalism.* Stockholm 1980.

Lundberg, E., *Svensk bostad.* Stockholm 1978 (1942).

———. *Byggnadskonsten i Sverige. Medeltid.* Stockholm 1940.

———. *Byggnadskonsten i Sverige. Sengotik, Renessans.* Stockholm 1948.

Mackeprang, M. *Vore landsbykirker.* Copenhagen 1944.

Millech, K. *Danske arkitekturstrømninger 1850–1950.* Copenhagen 1951.

Mårdh, P. A. *Röda stugor.* Stockholm 1990.

Neubert, G., Vibild, K. *Gamle Sjællandske bondehuse.* Køge 1975.

Neuenschwander, E. & C. *Atelier Alvar Aalto 1950–1951.* Zurich 1954.

Norberg-Schulz, C.: *Modern Norwegian Architecture.* Oslo 1986.

————. Arne *Korsmo.* Oslo 1986.

————. Scandinavia. *Architettura gli ultimi vent'anni.* Milan 1990.

————. Church at Bagsværd. *Global Architecture 61.* Tokyo 1981.

————. The Swiss Style. Blaser, W.: *Fantasie in Holz.* Basel 1987.

Nordin, E. *Svenska träkyrkor.* Stockholm 1965.

Norri, M. R., ed. *Pietilä.* Helsinki 1985.

Ohlmarks, Å., Bæhrendts, N. E. *Svenska krönikan.* Stockholm 1981.

Okkonen, O. *Finsk konst.* Porvoo and Helsinki 1946.

Pallasmaa, J., ed. *Lars Sonck.* Helsinki 1981.

————. Hvitträsk. Helsinki 1987.

Palm, B. *Arkitekten Carl Westman.* Lund 1954.

Paulsson, G. *Den nya arkitekturen.* Stockholm 1916.

Paulsson, T. *Scandinavian Architecture.* London 1957.

Pedersen, J. *Arkitekten Arne Jacobsen.* Copenhagen 1957.

Petterson, L. *Finnish Wooden Church.* Helsinki 1989.

Phleps, H. *Norwegische Stabkirchen.* Karlsruhe 1958.

Pihl Atmer, A. K. *Sommarnöjet i Skärgården.* Stockholm 1987.

Pitkänen, M. A., Souminen, T. *Suomalainen maisema.* Espoo 1977.

Quantrill, M. *Reima Pietilä.* New York 1985.

Quantrill, M., ed. *One Man's Odyssey in Search of Finnish Architecture.* Helsinki 1988.

Rasmussen, S. E. *Byer og bygninger.* Copenhagen 1949.

————. *Nordische Baukunst.* Berlin 1940.

Richards, J. M. *800 Years of Finnish Architecture.* London 1978.

Ringbom, S. *Stone, Style & Truth.* Helsinki 1987.

Ronglien, D., ed. *Treprisen 1961–1986.* Oslo 1988.

Romare, B., ed. *Verk av L. I. Wahlman.* Stockholm 1950.

Roosval, J. *Den baltiska Nordens kyrkor.* Uppsala 1924.

Roander, G., ed. *Knuttimring i Norden.* Falun 1986.

Rudberg, E. *Sven Markelius, arkitekt.* Stockholm 1989.

Råberg, P. G. *Funktionalistisk genombrott.* Stockholm 1970.

Schildt, G. *Det vita bordet.* Helsinki 1982.

————. Moderna tider. Helsinki 1985.

————. Den mänskliga faktorn. Helsinki 1990.

Schildt, G., ed. Alvar Aalto Skisser. Helsinki 1973.

Sihvo, P. *Tradition und Volkskunst in Finnland.* Helsinki 1978.

Skovgaard, J. *A King's Architecture.* London 1973.

Smidt, C. M. *Vor Frue Kirke.* Copenhagen 1980.

Stoklund, B. *Bondegård og byggeskik.* Copenhagen 1969.

Suomen Rakennustaidetta. Helsinki 1932.

Sverige, land och folk I–III. Stockholm 1966.

Sønderby, K., Gelsted, O., Marcus, Aa., Paludan, J., Smith, J., Stage, M. *Det danske land.* Copenhagen u.å.

Thiis-Evensen, T. *The Postmodernists Jan & Jon.* Oslo 1984.

Trettiotalets byggnadskonst i Sverige. Stockholm 1943.

Tschudi-Madsen, S. *Henrik Bull.* Oslo 1983.

Tuulse, A. *Romansk konst i Norden.* Stockholm 1968.

Tveten, A. S., Knutsen, B. E. *Knut Knutsen.* Oslo 1982.

Uppmark, G. *Svensk byggnadskonst 1530–1760.* Stockholm 1904.

Varnedoe, K. *Nordisk gullalderkunst.* Oslo 1987.

———. *Northern Light.* Brooklyn 1982.

Voss, K. *Arkitekten Nicolai Eigtved.* Copenhagen 1971.

Vreim, H. *Norsk trearkitektur.* Oslo 1947.

Weilbach, F. *Arkitekten Lauritz Thura.* Copenhagen 1924.

Wickberg, N. E. *Byggnadskonst i Finland.* Helsinki 1959.

———. Senaatintori. Rungsted Kyst 1981.

Wrede, S. *The Architecture of Erik Gunnar Asplund.* Cambridge, Mass. 1980.